Sweet *Is the* WORK

OTHER BOOKS
BY BREANNA OLAVESON

Mighty Miracles
The Perfect Gift

Sweet Is the WORK

LESSONS FROM THE FIRST SISTER MISSIONARIES

BREANNA OLAVESON

Covenant Communications, Inc.

For Lyla and Nora,
who were born for such a time as this

TABLE OF CONTENTS

ACKNOWLEDGMENTS

As always, I thank my husband, Ryan, for his inexhaustible love and support. Thanks for being our kids' best friend, for believing in me and in my dreams, and for staying excited about this book even in its mundane stages. I'm so glad we're partners.

Thanks also to my dad, who remains my favorite teacher and greatest critic, even in his retirement. Thank you for reading every draft I sent and for texting me ideas that made this book so much better. *Sweet Is the Work* wouldn't be what it is without your help, and I mean that literally since the title was also your idea.

I so appreciate everyone at Covenant Communications for making this book a reality. I especially thank my editor, Sam, for reading every word and improving every page, for encouraging me to tell these women's stories in the best possible way, and for answering most e-mails within minutes. I have no idea how you do that, but I love it. Thanks also to Angela for her help with artwork, and thanks to Margaret for answering her phone at 10:00 p.m. to discuss cover art. You are both shining stars, and I appreciate you so much.

Thank you to Rozanne Paxman, whom I met on the train after a long day of searching in vain for information about Katherine Love Paxman. It had to be fate. Thank you also to Katie McCue, who provided me with the Paxmans' digitized journals. I can't thank you enough for your help, and I hope you are happy with the way your ancestors' story is told in this book.

And finally, thank you to you, dear reader. I hope the stories of these amazing missionaries inspire you as much as they have inspired me.

Breanna

INTRODUCTION
The Errand of Angels

When I was nineteen years old, I asked my bishop if I could serve a mission. A friend in my ward was submitting his papers, and I couldn't see what was preventing me from doing the same while I still, in my estimation, had the freedom to do so. I was told in a kind and loving manner that I was not eligible until I turned twenty-one. To get an exception, I would have to discuss that rule with the prophet.

Like many other young women at that time, I met my husband before I was eligible for missionary service and had a bridal shower on my twenty-first birthday rather than a missionary send-off. I love the decision I made and have no regrets at all, but I still feel the missionary spirit and zeal.

On Saturday, October 6, 2012, during the first session of the 182nd Semiannual General Conference of The Church of Jesus Christ of Latter-day Saints, President Thomas S. Monson made a momentous announcement. He declared that the minimum age required for full-time missionary service would be decreased for both elders and sisters, effective immediately.

Elders, he said, were now eligible at age eighteen rather than nineteen. Sisters were now eligible at nineteen rather than twenty-one.

When I heard the announcement as I watched my nearly one-year-old daughter play on the floor, I felt a joy I had never before experienced. The opportunity I had wished for could be hers if she wanted it.

The impact of the announcement changed lives immediately. Many young women submitted their mission papers within days of the announcement. Clearly, they felt that age nineteen—before life decisions like finishing college, starting careers, and getting married became urgent—was an opportune time to serve in the mission field.

Consider how President Monson's announcement affected the missionary efforts of the Church statistically. At the end of 2011, the year prior to the announcement, 55,410 full-time missionaries were serving.[1] At the end of 2012, which included only three months of eligibility for these younger missionaries, the total had increased to 58,990. Of these missionaries, 8,100 were young women. By the end of 2013, when the bulk of those younger missionaries began their full-time service, the total jumped to 83,035—a 40-percent increase. Approximately 19,500 of these missionaries were young women—more than double the number of sisters who served the year before and about 23.4 percent of the total missionary force.[2] They served in 403 missions; in 2011, only 340 missions existed.

My niece Kalli received her mission call in March 2013, just a few months after that historic announcement. As I held my baby and watched Kalli open that long-awaited envelope, it occurred to me that my daughter and my niece had something in common—neither of their mothers had served as full-time missionaries. Who, I wondered, would they look to as role models in full-time missionary service?

That lingering question inspired this book. I found answers as I began my research. Even before the first full-time proselyting sister

---

1 See Hales, Brook P., "Statistical Report, 2011," *Ensign*, May 2012.

2 See Mormon Newsroom, "Thousands More Mormons Choose Missionary Service: Number of Female Missionaries Doubles; Process of Receiving a Mission Call Explained," Oct. 3, 2013; http://www.mormonnewsroom.org/article/thousands-more-mormons-choose-missionary-service; accessed January 19, 2016.

missionaries were officially called to England, approximately two hundred sisters served in unofficial capacities, often as companions to their husbands. As I learned about these women and read from their mission journals, I was inspired. I was taught. I was enriched. And I understood that every sister missionary shares this inspiring heritage.

With more young women serving as missionaries than have served in recent memory, many of these missionaries might feel they are blazing new trails, that perhaps they don't have a long-standing tradition of missionary service like the elders have. But they do. While sisters do not share the priesthood injunction to serve as missionaries, they have historically played a strong role in missionary efforts. And their successes began long before 1898 when the Church officially began calling young, single, female proselyting missionaries like those serving today.

For instance, Lucy Mack Smith, the Prophet Joseph's mother, was not called to proselyte but did so anyway. Her testimony was the catalyst for dozens of baptisms in Michigan. Christine Bentsen Anderson, a young convert from Denmark, taught Elder Erastus Snow his mission language before she and her family immigrated to Utah. Katherine Love Paxman's heart broke as she watched her baby girl die in the mission field. Eliza R. Snow was called to help pave the way for missionary efforts in Europe and the Holy Land. And Elizabeth Claridge McCune stood before hostile crowds to dispel anti-Mormon propaganda about the mistreatment of Mormon women in Utah.

The work of these women, among others, paved the way for the first sister missionaries to serve at the turn of the twentieth century. Today's missionary force is a testament to their success. Some of their stories—and so much more—are told in this book.

In many cases, I have used these missionaries' own words to tell their stories. Some errors in grammar, usage, and spelling remain in their personal journals and correspondence. In order to preserve their authentic voices, I have left many of these errors in the text of this book.

Learning from these outstanding sisters will inspire anyone who has an interest in missionary work today. I hope anyone who has read, "And ye shall go forth in the power of my Spirit, preaching my gospel, two by two, . . . declaring my word like unto angels of God"[3] and who believes that sometimes "the errand of angels is given to women"[4] will be as inspired as I have been.

Each of the missionaries in this book testified of Christ in different circumstances while facing difficult challenges. Each of their stories—one for every chapter of this book—teaches a profound truth from the past that can assist in missionary labors today. The results of these early sisters' efforts were excellent, and as we learn from their experiences, ours will be too.

---

3 Doctrine and Covenants 42:6.

4 See "As Sisters in Zion," *Hymns*, no. 309.

PROLOGUE
The Beginning of Something Great

ON MARCH 11, 1898, PRESIDENT Wilford Woodruff and his counselors, Joseph F. Smith and George Q. Cannon, gathered for their regularly scheduled leadership meeting.

Things were going well as The Church of Jesus Christ of Latter-day Saints neared its seventieth anniversary. The completion of the transcontinental railroad in 1869 had effectively ended the pioneer era of the Church and allowed new converts to travel to the Salt Lake Valley with relative ease. More than a quarter of a million Church members lived in forty stakes. The Book of Mormon had been translated into eleven languages. More than twelve thousand missionaries were currently serving in twenty missions worldwide.[5]

But the Church's growth brought its own challenges. It was difficult to coordinate the teaching and training of thousands of Church leaders in newly formed quorums and auxiliaries. The organizations' structures, curricula, activities, and meetings lacked consistency.[6] The Church was also struggling with its public image. Disaffected Church members were doing much damage to the Church, leading many people to incorrectly assume Mormons mistreated women.

5 See "A Look at the Church: 1844–1898," *Ensign*, August 1999.

6 See "Correlation of the Church Administration," in Daniel H. Ludlow, *Encyclopedia of Mormonism,* [1992], 1:323–25; http://eom.byu.edu/index.php/Correlation_of_the_Church_Administration.

On that day in 1898, the First Presidency discussed mostly routine matters. They determined how money should be distributed and reviewed which missionaries still needed to be set apart. It was an ordinary meeting in every way save one: the letters on the desk.

The First Presidency had received several letters from mission presidents around the world, all making the same unexpected request: more lady missionaries. Elder E. H. Nye, of the California Mission, suggested that "Elders in California who are soon to be released, might do much good by having their wives visit them and stay until their return, bearing their testimony and allaying prejudice."7

Elder Joseph W. McMurrin, of the European Mission, told success stories of women speaking to congregations in his mission: "[He] gave instances in which our sisters gained attention in England, where the Elders could scarcely gain a hearing. He believed that if a number of bright and intelligent women were called on missions to England, the results would be excellent."8

Finally, George Osmond, of the Star Valley Stake in Wyoming, wrote that a man in his stake, "called on a mission to the Northern States, was about to wed the daughter of [a bishop], and if they could go together, on their missions, being perfectly able and prepared, it would be a good thing."9

The First Presidency discussed the matter, raising a question both new and potentially controversial in the still-youthful church: Should women be routinely called as full-time missionaries?10

---

7 "Minutes from a meeting of the First Presidency," *Journal History of The Church of Jesus Christ of Latter-day Saints*, March 11, 1898, 2, Church Archives.

8 Ibid.

9 Ibid.

10 For some examples of prevailing opinions, see "Missionary Work for the Girls," *Young Woman's Journal* (October 1890), 29–30, Harold B. Lee Library, Brigham Young University, Provo, Utah.; http://contentdm.lib.byu.edu/cdm/compoundobject/collection/YWJ/id/9780/rec/2, and "Do You Believe in Lady Missionaries?" *Improvement Era*, Vol. 17, No. 1 (November 1915), 48–49.

Since the Church's infancy, priesthood holders had shouldered primary responsibility for preaching the gospel. When women did serve in the mission field, it was usually as supports to their husbands. However, as these letters proved, a few women in the mission field had been compelled to teach, to invite others to come to Christ, to testify in Christ's name, and to publicly defend the Church and its treatment of women. Each of these instances had been to the benefit of the Church.

It was a new idea and a potentially risky one. What would be the ramifications in the homes and in the settlements of Utah? But by the end of the meeting, it was decided that the man and his wife in Wyoming would both "receive a regular missionary call and certificate, and that it would be a good thing to call other sisters as occasion might require, to do missionary service."[11]

President George Q. Cannon made an official announcement at the 68th Annual General Conference of the Church in April 1898. He commented on the changing landscape of missionary work, then said, "It seems as though the Lord is preparing the way for the women of this Church to do some good in this direction. To some lands and under some circumstances suitable women might go with their husbands as missionaries and be able to do a great deal of good."[12]

President Joseph F. Smith spoke on the same topic some months prior to President Cannon's address, even before the 1898 First Presidency meeting. In November 1897, President Smith spoke to the Seventeenth Ward YLMIA, a precursor to today's Young Women

---

11 Minutes from a meeting of the First Presidency, *Journal History of the Church*, March 11, 1898, 2.

12 Cannon, George Q., "Address," in Conference Report, April 1898, 7; https:// archive.org/stream/conferencereport1898a/ onferencereport681chur#page/6/ mode/2up; accessed December 31, 2015.

organization.[13] He said, "We have, since the Church was organized, followed the practice of sending out Elders to preach the Gospel to the children of men. And for a great many years we followed in a rut—calling only men to perform this labor. We have thought that men only were able to preach the Gospel. But in later years, we have come to understand that the presence and testimony of an intelligent, faithful sister has, in certain cases, more weight than the testimony of many Elders. The testimony of women concerning their own condition accomplishes more good than that of a hundred men."[14]

In the official announcement in general conference, President Cannon told a story about a woman who resisted joining the Church, even though her husband was a member. She was acquainted with Mormon men but had heard rumors of oppressed Mormon women. When she finally met a Mormon woman, she found peace.

> The lady was so pleased at meeting one of our sisters—an intelligent woman, and a woman that did not look as though she was a poor, downtrodden slave—that she entered the Church. No doubt, it was due to the fact that she had found that the women were as intelligent, as presentable and as ladylike in their sphere as the gentlemen were in their sphere. This is encouraging, and it no doubt will enlarge our field of operations to a very great extent. There will be an opportunity, doubtless, for women who are capable and who desire to do good, to go out, under proper conditions.[15]

---

13 The source says this speech was given in November 1898, but as it was published in the February 1898 edition of the *Young Woman's Journal*, the date must be in error.

14 Smith, Joseph F., "Remarks of President Joseph F. Smith: Seventeenth Ward Y.L.M.I.A. November 30, 1898" *Young Woman's Journal*, Vol. 9 (February 1898), 84.

15 Cannon, George Q., "Address," in Conference Report, April 1898, 8.

He continued, addressing an unspoken concern. If women couldn't baptize, could they be missionaries? "Of course, they cannot administer the ordinances. It is not their province to officiate in the ordinances of the Gospel. But they can bear testimony; they can teach; they can distribute tracts, and they can do a great many things that would assist in the propagation of the Gospel of the Lord Jesus Christ."[16]

The first full-time, single, female proselyting missionaries of The Church of Jesus Christ of Latter-day Saints were set apart on April 1, 1898, and sent to the European Mission. Amanda "Inez" Knight and Lucy Jane Brimhall opened a new chapter of history for women in the Church.

But before they were called, two hundred other "bright and intelligent women"[17] had served in the mission field. They paved the way for Sister Knight, Sister Brimhall, and thousands of sisters since to answer the invitation of the Lord: "Those who desire in their hearts, in meekness, to warn sinners to repentance, let them be ordained unto this power."[18]

To understand the heritage these women left for all sister missionaries who came after them, one must start at the beginning.

---

16 Ibid.

17 Minutes from a meeting of the First Presidency, *Journal History of The Church of Jesus Christ of Latter-day Saints*, March 11, 1898, 2, Church Archives.

18 Doctrine and Covenants 63:57.

LUCY MACK SMITH

Portrait of Lucy Mack Smith by Lee Greene Richards © By Intellectual Reserve, Inc.

LESSON 1
Speak the Truth with Boldness

Lucy Mack Smith, the Prophet Joseph Smith's mother, was not formally called to preach the gospel in Michigan, but this fifty-six-year-old mother could not be restrained from sharing the gospel with others, even when the people around her were hesitant to discuss it.[19]

LUCY MACK SMITH SAT READING in her ship cabin. She was traveling with her son Hyrum, her niece Almira, fellow Church member John Murdock, and a few other missionaries of The Church of Jesus Christ of Latter-day Saints.[20] This ship would carry them from New York across Lake Erie to Detroit, where Lucy looked forward to visiting family. After spending some time in Michigan, the men would go on to Missouri while Lucy went to her new home in Kirtland, Ohio.

The elders' route had been determined by revelation, which has since been recorded in the Doctrine and Covenants. On June

---

19 Some scholars have disputed the accuracy of Lucy's memories of these events. Still, the text for this chapter was taken from her personal writings.

20 See Smith, Lucy, *Biographical Sketches of Joseph Smith the Prophet and His Progenitors for Many Generations* (Liverpool: Pratt and Richards, 1853), 186.

6, 1831, the Prophet Joseph Smith said in the Lord's name: "I, the Lord, will make known unto you what I will that ye shall do from this time until the next conference. . . . [Let] my servant John Murdock, and my servant Hyrum Smith, take their journey . . . by the way of Detroit."[21]

The Lord's commandment regarding the trip continued, advising the missionaries to "journey from thence preaching the word by the way, saying none other things than that which the prophets and apostles have written, and that which is taught them by the Comforter through the prayer of faith. Let them go two by two, and thus let them preach by the way in every congregation, baptizing by water, and the laying on of the hands by the water's side."[22] Lucy couldn't baptize, but she could preach, and she had difficulty refraining from doing so.

The commandment came in the shadow of tragedy. One month prior, on May 1, John Murdock's wife died shortly after giving birth to healthy twins. Emma Smith, Joseph's wife, had prematurely given birth to twins the day before; both twins had died. Joseph and Emma adopted the Murdock twins. The solution perhaps softened the blow of both tragedies, but John was still left a widower with three older children to care for. In a revelation given through Joseph for John, the Lord commanded John not to leave on his mission until he found someone to provide for his children while he was away.[23]

A month after this heartbreak, John and his companions—including Lucy Smith—left for Detroit. Although she wasn't called as a missionary, Lucy understood the commission of all baptized members of the Church to "stand as witnesses of God at all times and in all things, and in all places,"[24] as the newly published Book

---

21 Doctrine and Covenants 52:2, 8.

22 Doctrine and Covenants 52:9–10.

23 John Murdock's children are mentioned in Doctrine and Covenants 99:6.

24 Mosiah 18:9.

of Mormon in her hands taught. She was prepared to share the gospel if the opportunity arose. She didn't have to wait long.

Presently, a woman approached Lucy and asked what book she was reading.

"The Book of Mormon," Lucy replied.

The woman didn't recognize the title and asked Lucy to explain, so Lucy gave a brief history of the discovery and translation of the book. The woman was, to use Lucy's word, "delighted."[25]

"It is a record of the origin of the aborigines of America," Lucy added.

This seemed to interest the woman. "How I do wish that I could get one of your books to carry to my husband," she said. "He is now a missionary among the Indians."

But before the woman could tell Lucy which church her husband was a missionary for or where he was currently living, another woman approached. She was a doctor's wife, elegantly dressed with a satin scarf around her shoulders. As she walked, the scarf sometimes fell from her left shoulder and exposed a neck decorated with brilliant jewels. She carried herself daintily, but she frowned at the women as she approached. "I do not want to hear any more of that stuff, or anything more about Joe Smith either," she said. "They say that he is a Mormon prophet, but it is nothing but deception and lies. There was one man, Murdock, who believed in Joe Smith's doctrines. The Mormons all believe they can cure the sick and raise the dead. So when this Mr. Murdock's wife was sick, he refused to send for a doctor although the poor woman wanted him to do so. And so, by his neglect, his wife died."[26]

Lucy was well-acquainted with Elder Murdock's loss. She knew that to claim the death was a result of obstinate refusal to call a doctor was simply not true. Calling a doctor during childbirth was not common practice at the time, as midwives were generally the

---

25 *Biographical Sketches of Joseph Smith the Prophet and His Progenitors for Many Generations*, 186.

26 Ibid., 186–187.

preferred option to doctors, who frequently spread disease and who often had no specialized experience with obstetrics. In any case, hundreds of women died in childbirth every year. With or without a doctor, Julia's fate had likely been determined long before the time to call a doctor had arrived.

"I think you must be a little mistaken," Lucy said. "I am acquainted with the family and know something in regards to the matter."

"I know all about it," the woman said, raising her hand as though to wave aside Lucy's concern.

"Well now, perhaps not," Lucy said. "Just stop a moment, and I will explain it to you."

"No, I won't," she said.

"Then I will introduce you to Mr. Murdock and let him tell the story himself."

Lucy turned to John Murdock, who stood nearby. But just as Lucy began to introduce him, the woman's husband appeared and escorted her away. The conversation ended, but after that, The Church of Jesus Christ of Latter-day Saints was the most widely discussed topic on the boat.[27]

When they docked in Detroit, Lucy and her companions spent a night in a tavern to allow Almira's sister Lovisa Cooper time to "calm her nerves" before the party arrived at her home. Precisely what ailed Lovisa was unclear. They knew only that she was "exceedingly nervous"[28] and that she couldn't abide the thought of more than one visitor at a time.

Lucy was eventually allowed into Lovisa's room and showed little compassion for the girl's nerves. Lucy demanded that Lovisa allow the entire party to stay with her, and when Lovisa refused, Lucy spoke plainly. "Lovisa," she said. "Do you know what ails you? I can tell you exactly what it is. There is a good spirit and an evil one operating

---

27 Ibid, 187.

28 Ibid.

upon you, and the bad spirit has almost got possession of you. When the good spirit is the least agitated, the evil one strives for the entire mastery, and sets the good spirit to fluttering, just ready to be gone, because it has so slight a foothold. But you have been so for a long time, and you may yet live many years. These men who are with me are clothed with the authority of the Priesthood. Through their administration, you might receive a blessing. Even should you not be healed, do you not wish to know something about your Savior before you meet him?" If that wasn't enough incentive, Lucy ended with an ultimatum: "Furthermore, if you refuse to receive my brethren into your house, I shall leave it myself."[29]

So Lovisa agreed to host the men, along with her aunt, for dinner that night. The elders gave Lovisa two priesthood blessings before they left. In stark contrast to their initial meeting, Lovisa found that their company brought her joy, and she was distressed to see them go.

The morning after the elders left, Lucy and Almira set out for Pontiac to visit more family members. They visited Lucy's sister-in-law, who was staying with the woman's daughter's family. As seemed to happen frequently when people spoke to Lucy, the subject of religion came up almost immediately and remained the topic of discussion for quite some time. Lucy spoke of the restored gospel matter-of-factly, but her sister-in-law was not easily pacified.

She stood, saying, "Sister Lucy, you must excuse me. . . . I cannot bear conversation any longer. The subject is so entirely new, it confuses my mind."

"Please, stop a moment," Lucy said, remembering Lovisa's similarly agitated nerves. She rehearsed a similar speech to the one she had given Lovisa. "Suppose a company of fashionable people were to come in and begin to talk about balls, parties, and the latest style of making dresses, do you think that would agitate you so?"

---

29 Ibid., 188.

Sister Mack smiled. "I do not know that it would, sister Lucy; you know that those are more common things."

Lucy let the matter rest and resolved not to say more to her sister-in-law about religion unless she asked about it. Then, in the stillness of that night, just as they prepared for sleep, Lucy's sister-in-law asked her to teach her more about the gospel. Lucy obliged, and her sister-in-law was convinced of the truth of the gospel as she taught.[30]

A few days later, Lucy was again visiting family when someone introduced her to a local pastor named Mr. Ruggles. The pastor shook Lucy's hand and said, "You are the mother of that poor, foolish, silly boy, Joe Smith, who pretended to translate the Book of Mormon."

Lucy said, "I am, sir, the mother of Joseph Smith. But why do you apply to him such epithets as those?"

Missionaries in Michigan

Lucy Mack Smith was among the first missionaries in Michigan, even if her responsibilities were limited. After her visit, her sons Joseph and Hyrum visited the state with Oliver Cowdery, David Whitmer, Martin Harris, Frederick G. Williams, and Robert Orton. These men, as well as missionary Jared Carter, preached the gospel in the state in Lucy's wake.

By the early 1840s, the Church had more than twenty-five branches in the state. More were created in 1844, but after the martyrdom of Joseph and Hyrum in June of that year, many of the Saints in Michigan joined the westward trek with Brigham Young. Others joined splinter groups led by apostates and remained in Michigan. As a result of the beginning of the Civil War and the antagonistic efforts of the split-off groups, missionaries did not preach the gospel in Michigan again until the 1870s (see Deseret News 2013 Church Almanac [2012], 368–369).

---

30 Ibid., 189.

Mr. Ruggles told her it was because Joseph "should imagine he was going to break down all other churches with that simple Mormon book." But when Lucy asked if he had read it, he told her he had not.

"The scriptures say, 'Prove all things.' And now, sir, let me tell you boldly that that book contains the everlasting gospel and it was written for the salvation of your soul by the gift and power of the Holy Ghost."

"Nonsense," he said. "I am not afraid of any member of my church being led astray by such stuff. They have too much intelligence."

"Mr. Ruggles," Lucy said, speaking by the Spirit, for she felt it distinctly now. "Mark my words: As true as God lives, before three years we will have more than one third of your church. And, sir, whether you believe it or not, we will take the very deacon too."[31]

Lucy labored incessantly for the truth's sake and convinced many of the truth of the gospel during her time in Michigan. One man she became acquainted with, a "Mr. Cooper," observed that the Mormon missionaries might have more success if they dressed better.

When Lucy returned, she told Joseph what Mr. Cooper had said. He sent Jared Carter, who was dressed impressively in a superfine broadcloth suit, as a missionary to the area. He immediately went to Mr. Ruggles' church and baptized seventy of that church's members, including the deacon.[32]

---

31 Ibid., 190.

32 Ibid., 191.

ANN SOPHIA JONES ROSSER

LESSON 2
Take Every Opportunity to Share the Gospel

Ann Sophia Jones Rosser, a convert to the Church from Wales, participated actively in missionary work where she lived by participating in tract societies. She once distributed fifty tracts and sold seven copies of the Book of Mormon in one day, which reportedly led to twelve eventual baptisms. But even after her time with the tract societies was complete, she continued in missionary efforts.

Years after Lucy Mack Smith shared the gospel alongside the elders in Michigan, another woman undertook her own missionary labors half a world away. A Welsh woman named Ann Sophia Jones Rosser was nineteen years old when she was baptized and when she covenanted to "stand as a witness of God."[33] Her most famous chance came when Eli B. Kelsey, a Church leader in her area, introduced his plan.

Kelsey's goal was to establish tract societies that he hoped would distribute 25,000 tracts throughout the area. These small pieces of literature, usually leaflets or small booklets, were a popular way of spreading religious ideas in England at the time. They became so

---

33 Mosiah 18:9.

popular during the 1830s and 1840s that the movement, which aimed to effect change in the Church of England, became known as Tractarianism.[34]

In January 1851, Kelsey placed an order for thousands of tracts, and his approach worked. In April 1851, he reported:

> Since I wrote to you in January, between three and four hundred members have been added by baptism, and, according to the monthly reports of the presidents of branches and traveling elders, now coming in, the prospects are very bright indeed, for a far greater increase in the next three months. The number of tracts now in circulation in this Conference is twenty thousand; this number will be increased to over thirty thousand by the first of June. These silent messengers are generally well received, and have had a tendency to bring hundreds to the meetings who never came before.[35]

The large-scale effort derived its strength from individuals like Ann. Records of personal success were rare, but New York writer Edward Tullidge reported in 1877 that the Mormon women had at one time circulated five hundred thousand of Orson Pratt's tracts.[36]

Ann was a devoted part of these early tract societies. She didn't keep a record of her life, but stories of her success were legendary and even crossed the ocean to be retold in Salt Lake City. Elmer B.

---

34 See Philip Schaff, *New Schaff-Herzog Encyclopedia of Religious Knowledge,* Vol. XI: Son of Man–Tremellius, 479; http://www.ccel.org/ccel/schaff/encyc11/Page_479.html; accessed Dec. 28, 2015.

35 "A Communication from Elder Eli B. Kelsey," *The Latter-day Saints' Millennial Star,"* April 10, 1851, 140.

36 See Tullidge, Edward W. "Women of Mormondom" (New York, 1877), photo lithographic reprint of original edition, Salt Lake City, 1957, 276; https://archive.org/stream/womenofmormondom00tull#page/n7/mode/2up.

Tell Your Story

Unfortunately, we know very little about Ann Rosser. Her work with the tract societies has become, but when it comes to other details of her life—and even details about how she went about distributing tracts successfully—we are left to guess.

This is due mostly to the fact that Ann, like many other women at the time, left no record of her own life. Rebecca Bartholomew wrote the following in Audacious Women:

> *It was of no apparent concern to Ann Rosser that her contributions remained unacknowledged except as she became a legend in the hearts of local members. Yet one wonders why she was eighty-two before someone thought to honor her with a short biography in the* Millennial Star. . . .

> *Still one must ask why spiritual achievement should remain uncelebrated in a church which set itself apart from the world as accessible to all regardless of rank. In this regard at least—status accorded women—Mormons were like their contemporaries. It should be admitted that women themselves colluded in this negligence. Like Ann Rosser, most sisters did not leave records of their lives or works. Their own histories slight their youths, conversions, and branch experiences in their homeland. . . .*

> *Ironically then it is to clerks we turn for details about the British sisters: sporadic references in branch, conference and mission histories supplemented by obituaries in the* Millennial Star *and the sometimes-richly-detailed journals of male missionaries.* (Bartholomew, Rebecca, *Audacious Women: Early British Mormon Immigrants,* Chapter 4, "The Branches"; http://signaturebookslibrary.org/audacious-women-04/; accessed November 30, 2016)

Edwards wrote in *The Latter-day Saints' Millennial Star* that "in one day Sister Rosser distributed fifty tracts and sold seven copies of the Book of Mormon, which resulted in the conversion of twelve persons. She has also been instrumental in converting scores of others, and assisting many to emigrate to Utah."[37]

Ann's contributions to the tract societies were significant, but as Edwards indicated, her missionary efforts didn't stop there. For more than seventy years, she lived in England and served as a stalwart Church member. She hosted hundreds of missionaries in her home as well as six Church presidents: Brigham Young, Wilford Woodruff, John Taylor, Lorenzo Snow, Joseph F. Smith, and Heber J. Grant. The unnamed "scores of others" she helped convert to the gospel may not have recorded her name, but she had an eternal influence on them and on the generations who followed.

Ann witnessed a miracle when only one person out of several hundred living in her small town died in a deadly cholera epidemic. Another time, she and several elders of the Church were in a building when the ceiling fell in; none were injured. But perhaps the greatest miracle of her life was her ability to clean her own house and to walk three miles to do her weekly shopping even in her old age, a gift she attributed to careful observance of the Word of Wisdom.[38] She also once said that she "[had] beheld the workings of practically all the miraculous gifts of the spirit."[39]

The first full-time, single, female proselyting missionaries were sent to England in 1898, when Ann was sixty-four years old. She herself never received a formal mission call, but it was her life's mission to share the gospel by any means available to her. Today's missionaries emulate her example when they are obedient and, perhaps more impressively, when they continue in missionary endeavors long after their official sanctions are complete.

---

37 Edwards, Elmer B. "A Faithful Sister," *The Latter-day Saints' Millennial Star*, 278.

38 See Ibid.

39 Ibid.

LOUISA BARNES PRATT

Used by permission, Utah State Historical Society.

LESSON 3
The World Needs Each Missionary's Unique Gifts

*Louisa Barnes Pratt supported her family at home for years while
her husband, Addison, served as a missionary on the Society
Islands (known today as French Polynesia, near Tahiti). When she
was called to join him, Louisa gathered her four daughters and
prepared to serve faithfully as a missionary herself. She soon
learned that the native people on the island of Tubuai
needed her practical skills and gospel knowledge.*

LOUISA BARNES PRATT WAS FULLY capable of acting as both bread-
winner and nurturer to her four daughters. She proved it during the
five years she spent without her husband, Addison, while he served
as a missionary on the Society Islands.

Of course, it wasn't unusual for women in the early days of the
Church to face challenges while their husbands were away on missions or filling other Church assignments. What made Louisa's story
different was that the Lord used these hardships as a kind of refiner's
fire, as preparation for her own mission call that changed the lives of

hundreds of native Pacific islanders. During her mission, she taught, preached, and even healed the sick.[40]

But before the mission came the challenge of providing for, nurturing, and raising her children alone in the nineteenth century.

When Joseph Smith called Addison and three other men to serve as missionaries in the Pacific, Louisa was left in a difficult position. The Pratts' oldest daughter, Ellen, was eleven years old. Their youngest daughter was three. Louisa and Addison had been members of the Church for just five years, having arrived in Nauvoo two years prior to Addison's departure. In short, Addison's mission call in 1843 might have been considered premature by today's standards. But he faithfully embarked on his mission "without purse or scrip"[41] and left Louisa with little more—just the land they had purchased in Nauvoo, her skills as a seamstress, and her knack for driving a hard bargain. Several men in Nauvoo promised Addison they would look after her, but ultimately, none followed through.

It was uncommon in 1843 for women, whether inside or outside the Church, to provide economically for their families. However, with many men called on full-time missions great distances from their families, women like Louisa were doing what many considered impossible: the work of both a woman and a man. Louisa worked as a seamstress and undertook primary responsibility for their home and family in Addison's absence.

---

40 For important historical context regarding women who gave blessings of healing, see "Joseph Smith's Teachings about Priesthood, Temple, and Women," *Gospel Topics,* LDS.org, 2016. In part, the essay reads, "During the 19th century, women frequently blessed the sick by the prayer of faith, and many women received priesthood blessings promising that they would have the gift of healing. . . . In reference to these healing blessings, Relief Society general president Eliza R. Snow explained in 1883, 'Women can administer in the name of JESUS, but not by virtue of the Priesthood.'"

41 Perrin, Kathleen C., "Louisa Barnes Pratt: Self-Reliant Missionary Wife," *Go Ye into All the World: The Growth & Development of Mormon Missionary Work,* ed. Reid L. Nielson and Fred E. Woods (Provo, UT: Religious Studies Center, 2012), 261–88. https://rsc.byu.edu/archived/go-ye-all-world/missionary-work-asia-and-pacific-isles/11-louisa-barnes-pratt-self-reliant#_ednref47; accessed Dec. 29, 2015.

Louisa later wrote in her journal: "My four children had to be schooled and clothed, and no money would be left with me. In those days nearly everything was trade; making it more difficult for a mother to be left to provide for herself and children. My heart felt weak at the first, but I determined to trust in the Lord, and stand bravely before the ills of life, and rejoice that my husband was counted worthy to preach the gospel."[42]

For Louisa, life in Nauvoo provided sufficient difficulty to keep her occupied. But on June 27, 1844, her situation became much worse.

The martyrdom of the Prophet Joseph Smith and his brother Hyrum left the Saints without a leader and without much direction. Addison was still thousands of miles away, and Louisa had her four children—now ages twelve, ten, seven, and four—to think about. The Saints were heading west, and Louisa knew she must join them. She received her endowment in the newly completed Nauvoo Temple before embarking on the potentially hazardous journey.

She joined a company made up mostly of women and children for the journey west, and though she became ill at Winter Quarters, she eventually made her way to the Salt Lake Valley with all her children. Addison met his family in Utah one week after their arrival. Their youngest daughter, now eight years old, didn't recognize him.[43]

But the family's time together in their new home was brief. In 1849, just a year after they settled in Salt Lake, Addison left for his second mission to the Pacific. This time, Louisa would join him. She was prepared to answer the Lord's call to be a missionary herself. She and the girls left in 1850 with Louisa's sister, Caroline Crosby.

Though it was not common practice at the time, Louisa was blessed and set apart before her mission. Of the experience, she wrote:

---

42 Pratt, Louisa Barnes, *Mormondom's First Woman Missionary: Life Story and Travels Told in Her Own Words,* (Daughters of Utah Pioneers), ed. Kate B. Carter, 228.

43 "Louisa Barnes Pratt: Self-Reliant Missionary Wife," 358–59.

Brother [Brigham] Young blessed me. He said I was called, set apart, and ordained to go to the Islands of the sea to aid my husband in teaching the people. That I should be honored by those with whom I travelled, that all my wants should be supplied, that no evil should befall me on the journey, that I should lack nothing, I should have power to rebuke the Destroyer from my house, that he should not have power to remove any of my family; that I should do a good work, and return in peace; many other things, all of which he sealed upon my head in the name of the Lord.[44]

Equal Partners

Louisa Barnes Pratt was an effective missionary. Her husband, Addison, was also an incredibly successful missionary and a fitting companion for Louisa, even if the two of them ultimately spent little time together in the mission field.

Years prior to his baptism, in the early 1820s, Addison lived in the Society and Sandwich Islands (today's French Polynesia and Hawaii) as a member of a ship's crew. He fell in love with the islands—the people, the climate, and the beauty of the landscape—so when he learned about the Church's missionary efforts after his baptism, Addison asked if he could serve a mission there. He and other missionaries left for the islands and eventually made a stop in Tubuai to obtain fresh food on April 29, 1844.

His journal says, "The king and chiefs were quite anxious that one of us should stay on the island. I was soon convinced that should I leave this island I would be running away from duty and resolved at once to stay here" (Pratt, Louisa Barnes, *Mormondom's First Woman Missionary: Life Story and Travels Told in Her Own Words*, (Daughters of Utah Pioneers, ed. Kate B. Carter, 399).

So Addison stayed. It was the beginning of a lifetime of missionary service on the islands for both Addison and Louisa.

---

44 Pratt, Louisa Barnes, *Mormondom's First Woman Missionary: Life Story and Travels Told in Her Own Words,* (Daughters of Utah Pioneers), ed. Kate B. Carter, 252.

Because of this setting apart, Louisa is believed to be the first female missionary called and set apart to fill a mission. However, she is not typically considered the "first female missionary" because she was called as an assistant to her husband and not as an independent proselyting missionary.[45]

Louisa and her daughters disembarked on the island of Tubuai on October 21, 1850. By now, her oldest child was eighteen and her youngest ten. Louisa was forty-eight.

Addison was not there when Louisa and his children arrived. He was held up in Tahiti trying to resolve misunderstandings with the government.

His delay set the tone for Louisa's mission. Though she was called to assist her husband in his work, she and her daughters were often on their own. Fortunately, they had lived independently before.

The islands Louisa and her family now called home were familiar with Christian missionaries. Beginning in the late eighteenth century, European missionaries traveled to the islands and brought their religions—and their diseases—with them. The population on the islands was now significantly smaller than it had been in decades prior.[46] Even so, the Mormon missionaries were well received. Addison's first baptism happened less than two months after his initial arrival on the islands. Five weeks later, ten more people—five white and five native—were baptized.[47]

---

45 See Kunz, Calvin S., "A History of Female Missionary Activity in The Church of Jesus Christ of Latter-day Saints, 1830–1898," (master's thesis, Brigham Young University, 1976), 18–22; http://scholarsarchive.byu.edu/cgi/viewcontent.cgi?article=5857&context=etd; accessed December 3, 2016.

46 Louisa recorded her firsthand experience with this decrease in population. She wrote, "There is a disease prevalent in the islands not known before the whites came among them" (Louisa Barnes Pratt, *Mormondom's First Woman Missionary: Life Story and Travels Told in Her Own Words*, (Daughters of Utah Pioneers), ed. Kate B. Carter, 276). Also see *Journal of Voyages and Travels by the Rev. Daniel Tyerman and George Bennet, Esq*, compiled by James Montgomery (Frederick Westley and A. H. Davis 1831), 75.

47 See *Deseret News 2013 Church Almanac* (2012), 480.

Six years later, Louisa's arrival was also well received. Her skills and talents, once simply necessary for her survival, were valued commodities. She became a great teacher among the natives, sharing both her practical skills and her spiritual knowledge.

First, she learned the language. Her daughters learned more quickly than she did, but Louisa was diligent in her study. She wrote, "I am also advancing fast in a knowledge of the language. . . . Past the meridian of life, I learned a new language!"[48]

Once able to communicate sufficiently, Louisa taught the people what they wanted to know. An eternal feminist, she especially reached out to the women. She wrote, "I taught the women to knit; Some of the old men came & wanted to learn, so I learned them to knit suspenders, of the yarn I took from California. For needles we used the stem of the cocoanut leaf, which answered a good purpose. The women were very teachable in learning any thing I attempted to teach them."[49]

Louisa and Caroline Crosby, who accompanied Louisa on her mission, also taught school to the children on the island. On school days, they taught the island children classes in reading, English, mathematics, music, and religion until noon. After these school sessions, Caroline and Louisa taught their own children. They also taught skills to the native children's mothers. In addition to knitting, they taught classes in music, nursing, gardening, childcare, cleaning, etiquette, homemaking skills, quilting, and sewing. These skills were commonplace among the Saints in the United States, but on the islands, they were poorly understood domestic arts.

---

48 Pratt, Louisa Barnes, *Mormondom's First Woman Missionary: Life Story and Travels Told in Her Own Words,* (Daughters of Utah Pioneers), ed. Kate B. Carter, 274.

49 Pratt, Louisa Barnes, "Reminiscences," 78–80, 81–82, Church Archives. Quoted in Brittany Chapman, "'Capable of 'Great Good': Louisa Barnes Pratt Nurtured Saints in French Polynesia," (June 30, 2012). http:// history.lds.org/article/louisa-barnes-pratt-missionary?lang=eng; accessed May 29, 2014.

About one experience with teaching, Louisa wrote: "This morning I went to Mr. Layton's, who has a Tahitian wife, and she knows nothing about housekeeping. A young girl lives with them who assists in the cooking. I was very anxious to give her some instructions in the system of cleaning house and keeping it in order. I introduced the subject in a plausible manner so as not to offend. The young girl readily acquiesced seeming to believe it would be a nice affair to know how to keep house like 'mau tamahine papa,' foreign girls. It was astonishing the amount of rubbish we hoed out of one room."[50]

These skills were precious to the island women but not as valuable as the spiritual gifts the American women brought with them. In the nineteenth century, it was not uncommon for women to give blessings of healing. Joseph Smith taught, "Respecting the female laying on hands . . . it is no sin for any body to do it that has faith."[51] Many faithful women gave blessings of healing "in the name of JESUS, but not by virtue of the Priesthood," as Eliza R. Snow clarified.[52] In the twentieth century, Church leaders taught that Church members should instead follow the counsel in the New Testament to "call for the elders,"[53] who had authority to administer to the sick.

But as was appropriate in her day, Louisa brought with her a vial of oil that Brigham Young had consecrated. She used it to treat illnesses, though her precise methods are unclear. She blessed some by the laying on of hands and also by giving them a bit of oil to ingest. In all cases, she taught the people that they would be healed according to their faith. One experience related in Louisa's

---

50 Pratt, Louisa Barnes, *Mormondom's First Woman Missionary: Life Story and Travels Told in Her Own Words,* (Daughters of Utah Pioneers), ed. Kate B. Carter, 2743.

51 "Discourse, 28 April, as reported by Eliza R. Snow," (1842); available at josephsmithpapers.org.

52 Morgan Utah Stake Relief Society Minutes and Records, 1878–1973, Church Archives, April 28, 1883, 88. Quoted in "Joseph Smith's Teachings about Priesthood, Temple, and Women," *Gospel Topics,* LDS.org, 2016.

53 James 5:14.

journal describes how she acted as a physician on her mission: "An elderly woman came to me in the night, wished me to see a sister of hers who was very sick. I arose from my bed and went with her. She led me over an intricate dark woody place but I feared nothing. I told her she should be better in the morning, and so it proved. 'According to thy faith be it unto thee.' Consecrated oil which we brought from home has been blessed to their use often, all on account of the faith they have in it."[54]

Most important to her call as a missionary, however, was Louisa's work in preaching the gospel. She knew the scriptures and was well versed in their doctrines. As one historian wrote, "Louisa was often called upon to preach and answer gospel questions. She delved into such diverse topics as God's corporeal form, baptism for the dead, and Daniel's vision. To a group of visiting women, Louisa spoke of the Book of Mormon, which had not yet been translated into Tahitian. . . . Whether this view was spoken or not, Louisa was seen as the missionary leader in the absence of the elders, and her residence was referred to as the mission home."[55]

Louisa's daughter Ellen was also an eloquent Tahitian speaker and an effective teacher. Louisa wrote, "Ellen succeeds admirably well in expounding scripture to their understanding, showing her knowledge of the Bible and Book of Mormon, far exceeding my highest anticipations."[56]

---

54 Pratt, Louisa Barnes, *Mormondom's First Woman Missionary: Life Story and Travels Told in Her Own Words,* (Daughters of Utah Pioneers), ed. Kate B. Carter, 275.

55 Perrin, Kathleen C., "Louisa Barnes Pratt: Self-Reliant Missionary Wife," in *Go Ye into All the World: The Growth & Development of Mormon Missionary Work*, ed. Reid L. Nielson and Fred E. Woods (Provo, UT: Religious Studies Center, 2012), 261–88. https://rsc.byu.edu/archived/go-ye-all-world/missionary-work-asia-and-pacific-isles/11-louisa-barnes-pratt-self-reliant; accessed Nov. 19, 2016.

56 Pratt, Louisa Barnes, *Mormondom's First Woman Missionary: Life Story and Travels Told in Her Own Words,* (Daughters of Utah Pioneers), ed. Kate B. Carter, 275.

During their mission, the Pratts and those serving with them were required to abide by strict rules enacted by the French government. By 1852, the mission in French Polynesia was closed due to governmental restrictions. The Pratts returned to Salt Lake City that year, but their influence in French Polynesia lived on. Missionary work resumed in the country in 1892. Today, more than 25,000 members of the Church live in French Polynesia and reside in ninety congregations. They now have a temple, the Papeete Tahiti Temple, which was dedicated in 1983.[57]

Louisa Barnes Pratt's mission stands as a testament that the world needs what faithful disciples of Christ have to offer. Louisa knew the gospel enabled God's children to do more than they could on their own. Her reflections in her journal near the end of her mission reveal the blessings of the gospel she experienced and shared with the people on the islands: "This is the 21st anniversary of my marriage day. More than one third of that time I have lived a widow, or worse, alone, while my husband was on the opposite side of the globe. Cold and cruel as my fate sometimes appeared, the fullness of the Gospel as revealed in Latter Days, seemed a balm for all my woes. I could sing myself to sleep when not a morsel of bread was in my house, nor means to buy any, but I knew the promises of God were sure and that deliverance would come in time to save me and my children from hunger."[58]

---

57 See Mormon Newsroom, Facts and Statistics, "French Polynesia" (2016); http://www.mormonnewsroom.org/facts-and-statistics/country/french-polynesia; accessed September 2016.

58 Pratt, Louisa Barnes, *Mormondom's First Woman Missionary: Life Story and Travels Told in Her Own Words,* (Daughters of Utah Pioneers), ed. Kate B. Carter, 288.

CHRISTINE BENTSEN

Christine Bentsen is on the left.

PH 1700 3890_f0001_i0001_00001.JPG, courtesy of the Church History Library, The Church of Jesus Christ of Latter-day Saints

LESSON 4
If You Have a Testimony, You Have Enough

*Christine Bentsen was still a new convert when she became
involved in missionary work. Her commitment to the gospel, her
love for her family, and her desire to embark in missionary labors
laid the foundation for her success. As she helped her family
accept the gospel and as she taught one missionary to speak her
native language, she proved that if you have a testimony, you
have enough to be a successful missionary.*

CHURCH MEMBERS FREQUENTLY PRAY FOR the Spirit to touch the
hearts of world leaders and to prepare the way for missionaries to
preach the gospel in countries around the world. Sometimes, answers to those prayers are manifested clearly.

For example, King Frederik VII signed the Danish Constitution in 1849, guaranteeing religious freedom to Scandinavia.[59]
Later that year, at the October 1849 general conference, Elder Erastus Snow was assigned to establish the Church in Scandinavia, and
Peter O. Hansen, a Church member and native of Copenhagen,
was called to serve as a missionary in Denmark. John E. Forsgren,
a convert from Sweden, was also granted his request to be called
to the work. The three men arrived in Denmark in the spring of
1850.[60]

---

59 See "Highlights of the Church in Scandinavia," *Ensign*, July 1974.

60 See *Deseret News 2013 Church Almanac* (2012), 468.

Surely the Lord had prepared the way for the pure in heart among the Danish people to receive the gospel. Christine Bentsen was among them.

Christine had trained as a dressmaker and tailor on her home island of Bornholm, Denmark,[61] and was living in Copenhagen when the missionaries arrived.[62] She believed the missionaries were sent from God to teach her about Christ's restored church and was baptized on August 24, 1850, not two weeks after the first converts in Denmark were baptized on August 12.

She was the second person from Bornholm to be baptized. By the next year, the elders had organized a branch in her hometown. A Danish translation of the Book of Mormon, which Elder Hansen had begun while living in Nauvoo and completed in Salt Lake, was published that same year; it was the first time the Book of Mormon was published in a language other than English.

Christine became one of the first single women to be called as a missionary as the Church gained traction in Denmark. Because the Church apparently intended for her calling to be fulfilled by supporting the missionaries in logistical ways, she is not usually

> ## Where Women Served
>
> *Between 1830 and 1898, more than two hundred LDS women were involved in some type of missionary work. They served all over the world but more frequently in certain areas than in others. Here's where the most women performed missionary labors prior to 1898:*
>
> - *United States: California, New York, Michigan, Northwestern States, Colorado*
> - *Outside the US: Hawaiian Islands, England*

---

61 Jenson, Andrew, *Latter-day Saint Biographical Encyclopedia* (1941), Vol. 1, 507.

62 Gardner, Hamilton, *History of Lehi Including a Biographical Section, Deseret News* 1913, 331; *https://archive.org/stream/historyoflehiinc00gardrich# page/330/mode/2up/search/christine*+anderson; accessed Nov. 19, 2016.

regarded as the Church's first single female full-time missionary.[63] Nevertheless, through the capable way she fulfilled her calling, she still taught many people, including her own family, about Christ's restored church.

Elder Erastus Snow asked Christine to accompany two elders back to Bornholm to "help them in their work, by finding a home for them and assisting them otherwise."[64] She secured housing for the missionaries in her parents' house, then "assist[ed] them otherwise" by providing financial aid and by "prepar[ing] the way for them, in many instances, to preach the gospel."[65] She also helped Erastus Snow become a more effective missionary, taking "great pleasure in helping to teach the Danish language to [him]."[66]

By December 1852, most of Christine's family had been baptized and was preparing to immigrate to the United States. They left Denmark on December 20, all arriving in Utah in 1853, except for her father, who was in an accident and arrived the following year.[67]

Christine joined the Church with comparatively little understanding of its doctrines and history. Unlike some pioneer women who lived in the United States and personally heard Joseph Smith teach, Christine relied on the teachings of the missionaries and the whisperings of the Spirit to help her know the truth. But those things were enough.

---

63 Kunz, Calvin S., "A History of Female Missionary Activity in The Church of Jesus Christ of Latter-day Saints, 1830–1898," (master's thesis, Brigham Young University, 1976), 51–52; http://scholarsarchive.byu.edu/cgi/viewcontent.cgi?article=5857&context=etd.

64 Jenson, Andrew, *Latter-day Saint Biographical Encyclopedia* (1941), Vol. 1, 507.

65 Ibid.

66 Gardner, Hamilton, *History of Lehi Including a Biographical Section, Deseret News* 1913, 331; *https://archive.org/stream/historyoflehiinc00gardrich#page/330/mode/2up/search/christine*+anderson; accessed Nov. 19, 2016.

67 See Jenson, Andrew, *Latter-day Saint Biographical Encyclopedia* (1941), Vol. 1, 507.

She is proof that if a person has a testimony—if she knows Christ lives, that this Church is His restored church, and that His prophet speaks today—she has enough to be a successful missionary.

MILDRED E. RANDALL

LESSON 5
You Are Fully Capable of Fulfilling Your Mission

Mildred E. Randall was called to serve as a missionary with her husband, but when Alfred unexpectedly returned home early, Mildred was on her own. She completed her mission confidently and successfully and even returned to the mission field later as the first woman called independent of her husband. From her experience, we learn that the Lord qualifies each missionary to fulfill his or her assigned mission.

THE LORD PREPARED THE WAY for Mildred Randall to serve as a missionary, and she prepared the way for generations of sisters to serve confidently after her.

About forty-five years prior to Mildred's arrival on the Sandwich Islands, missionaries from Puritan New England arrived. They helped establish a written alphabet for the Hawaiian language, which enabled the native Hawaiian population to read and write in their own language.[68] Their positive influence warmed native Hawaiians to American missionaries.

During King Kamehameha III's reign from 1825–1854, he helped prepare his country for missionary work. The king was a

---

68 See "Hawaiian standardized as a written language," HawaiiHistory. org (2016); http://www.hawaiihistory.org/index.cfm?fuseaction=ig. page&PageID=280; accessed January 18, 2016.

Christian, and under his reign, Hawaii changed from an absolute monarchy to a Christian constitutional monarchy. He encouraged and actively helped missionary efforts. In fact, he wrote a letter in 1852 for Christian missionaries who were leaving Hawaii for Micronesia. It bore his official seal and was addressed to rulers of the various Pacific Islands. It read, in part:

> There are about to sail for your islands some teachers of the Most High God, Jehovah, to make known unto you His Word for your eternal salvation. . . . I commend these good teachers to your esteem and friendship and exhort you to listen to their instructions. I have seen the value of such teachers. We here on my islands lived once in ignorance and idolatry. We were given to war and were very poor. Now my people are enlightened. We live in peace and some have acquired property. Our condition is greatly improved and the Word of God is the cause of our improvement. I advise you to throw away your idols, take the Lord Jehovah for your God, worship and love Him and He will bless and save you.[69]

In 1849, some sixteen years prior to Mildred's arrival, Hawaii and the United States concluded a treaty of friendship. This treaty marked the beginning of official relations between the two parties.[70] So it was that in 1865, when Mildred arrived in Hawaii with Alfred on an LDS mission, she entered a fundamentally religious, pro-American, missionary-friendly environment.

---

69 Crawford, David and Leona, *Missionary Adventures in the South Pacific*, Charles E. Tuttle Company, Inc., 1967.

70 See U.S. Department of State, "Annexation of Hawaii"; http://future. state.gov/when/timeline/1866_timeline/annex_hawaii.html; accessed January 18, 2016.

Forever a Missionary

Long after her official release from missionary service, Mildred E. Randall took her responsibility to share the gospel seriously. The Deseret Evening News *printed the following letter from her, dated January 17, 1870, and noted that "her missionary experience seems to be of a more felicitous character than that of many of the brethren in the East":*

Prest. George A. Smith: —Dear Bro. — A few weeks since I wrote to you to send me several copies of the 'Voice of Warning.' There is, at the present time, much interest in 'Mormonism' manifest by the people here. . . .

I feel to rejoice greatly at the prospect before me; a good work is being begun here, and I hope will continue till all the honest in heart will learn the truth and obey it and be gathered out of Babylon. When I first arrived here I felt somewhat discouraged, the people were so ignorant of our religion and so much prejudiced against us that they did not want to hear anything about the 'Mormons,' considering us no better than heathen. I do not mean that every one was so, but the majority were. I have lost no time in speaking to my relatives and others of the principles of the everlasting gospel whenever an opportunity is presented. Now, wherever I go all are inquiring about us—what we believe in, what kind of society we have, our government, laws, etc. When I tell them that we believe in the Bible, they wonder at it, for they thought we rejected it. . . . The object of my visit was to do good to my friends, and the Lord has blessed my labors abundantly. I am feeling first-rate and know that the Holy Spirit is with me all the time. (Journal History of the Church, January 17, 1870)

But welcoming environment notwithstanding, Mildred and Alfred encountered some difficulty a few months after their arrival. Ultimately, Alfred decided to leave the islands and set sail for the United States for reasons not entirely known. The question was whether Mildred would join him.

The couple had lost two children in infancy not long before their call to serve. Francis died in November 1864 at twenty months old, and Eli, who was born less than two months after Francis's death, died of inflammation of the lungs a month after his birth.[71] Mildred tragically had no children to care for now.

She was a well-known schoolteacher in Salt Lake City who had taught in the private family school of Brigham Young. She had also taught grade school before her mission. But teaching school—presumably the thing most likely to draw her back to Utah—was precisely what had brought her to Hawaii in the first place. While Alfred had been assigned to help manage the Church plantation at Laie, Mildred had been assigned to teach school.[72]

She was committed to continuing the work she had started on the islands and remained behind when her husband left. In doing so, she became the first woman in Church history to serve as a full-time missionary without her husband.

For more than thirty years, Mildred's missionary situation was the exception; there were no other full-time female missionaries who served without their husbands. Some women served as part-time missionaries without their husbands, but usually these sisters had some other purpose for their mission, like genealogical research or higher education.[73]

---

71 See Boyce, Mildred Moss, *Mildred Eliza Johnson Randall* (March 1979), Church Archives, MS 10528, 4.

72 Ibid.

73 See Kunz, Calvin S., "A History of Female Missionary Activity in The Church of Jesus Christ of Latter-day Saints, 1830–1898," (master's thesis, Brigham Young University, 1976), 51–52; http://scholarsarchive.byu.edu/cgi/viewcontent.cgi?article=5857&context=etd.

Mildred was driven to help the Church schools in Hawaii succeed and found great satisfaction in doing so during her mission, which lasted for eighteen months. However, as time passed and she heard from Alfred only occasionally, she felt the pains that came from marital stress. Reflecting on this time, she wrote: "I . . . wished to remain, and do all the good I could for the mission, until those who sent me should call me home. He [Alfred] wrote to me a few times during my stay. I began to feel that I was, like his mission, forsaken and deserted."[74]

The first school Mildred opened in Hawaii was primarily for native children. She began with nine in her class: six were native Hawaiians, and three were children of white missionaries. As her classes steadily grew, Mildred eventually opened a second school that operated in English and was primarily for non-native children.[75]

She wrote: "In about six months my school began to increase in numbers and interest, and continued to do so up to the time I left. The children who have attended the school, during the three years, have improved very much in their English studies. They are quick to learn, and their memories are excellent to retain what they learn."[76]

When Mildred was released from her mission, President Brigham Young expressed his personal gratitude for her determination to serve

---

74 Mildred E. Randall to Brigham Young (November 8, 1875), Church Archive, 2–3. In the original text, Mildred put "like his mission" in parentheses. Parentheses have been changed to commas in this text to clarify that the words are hers. Quoted in Kunz, Calvin S., "A History of Female Missionary Activity in The Church of Jesus Christ of Latter-day Saints, 1830–1898," (master's thesis, Brigham Young University, 1976), 70; http://scholarsarchive.byu.edu/cgi/viewcontent.cgi?article=5857&context=etd.

75 See Kunz, Calvin S., "A History of Female Missionary Activity in The Church of Jesus Christ of Latter-day Saints, 1830–1898," (master's thesis, Brigham Young University, 1976), 51–52; http://scholarsarchive.byu.edu/cgi/viewcontent.cgi?article=5857&context=etd.

76 Mildred E. Randall to Brigham Young (September 16, 1876), Church Archive, 2. Quoted in "A History of Female Missionary Activity in The Church of Jesus Christ of Latter-day Saints, 1830–1898," 61.

to the end even when her husband did not: "Your faithfulness and diligence in staying there after your partner returned home and doing all the good that you could to benefit the people and help the mission is appreciated, and we feel to bless you therefor."[77]

Mildred completed her first mission in 1866. Seven years later, she made history when she became the first woman called to serve a mission independent of her husband, though unlike those women called in 1898, she was not called to proselyte. The Church needed Mildred's help in Hawaii yet again. This time, Alfred wasn't called to go with her.

In a letter, she confided her feelings to her sister Mary

Church Plantation at Laie

Laie was a gathering place on the islands for the Saints for whom it was impractical to immigrate to Salt Lake. As a first attempt at creating a gathering place, the Church established the "City of Joseph" on the island of Lanai in 1854. That attempt failed because of several factors, including the personal ambitions of adventurer Walter Murray Gibson. Gibson, a new convert to the Church, came to Hawaii in 1861 and essentially ran the Church as his "personal political kingdom" until 1864, when he was excommunicated for introducing false doctrines and for selling offices in the priesthood (See "Hawaii, the Church in," in Ludlow, Daniel *H.*, Encyclopedia of Mormonism, (1992); http://eom.byu.edu/index.php/Hawaii,_the_Church_in; accessed Nov. 19, 2016).

After that disastrous attempt at establishing a gathering place, Brigham Young sent two other missionaries to Hawaii to purchase property. This time, the Church bought a 6,000-acre plantation in Laie for $14,000 (Ibid.). *Laie became the center of LDS activities in Hawaii and, today, is home to a temple, a Church university, and the Polynesian Cultural Center.*

---

77 Letter to Mildred E. Randall from Brigham Young. In "Mildred Eliza Johnson Randall," MS 10528, Church Archives, 7.

Jane: "I do not feel at all discouraged. I am on a foreign mission, and the first woman who has ever been sent on such a mission without her husband. I consider it a great privilege and shall endeavor to do all the good I can while here. Have no idea how long I shall remain. Recently, my school has increased in numbers, and as teaching is my particular portion of the mission work here, I feel more encouraged."[78] Enrollment in Mildred's schools increased during her second mission, which lasted more than three years.

She knew the exhilaration of professional success and the loneliness of marital struggle. She excelled in her profession and dedicated her time and talents to the work of the Lord. She truly served Him with all her heart, might, mind, and strength. Like Church members today, she was capable of everything the Lord required of her and more. Even after nearly five combined years in the mission field, she was ready and willing to do more.

She later wrote: "I can truly say that all my labors connected with the Sandwich Islands mission have been pleasant. the time seemed to pass very rapidly, never allowed myself to feel discontented or homesick, and I know that I have been greatly benefited by it. Have learned lessons of economy, patience and perseverence which I could not have learned anywhere else . . . and if it is ever necessary for me to return to the Islands again, I shall be ready and willing to respond to the call."[79]

---

78 Mildred Randall to Mary Jane Johnson Eakle (February 16, 1873) [date appears to be in error; likely 1874], Church Archive, MS 3512, 2.

79 Mildred E. Randall to Brigham Young (September 16, 1876), 3–4. Quoted in "A History of Female Missionary Activity in The Church of Jesus Christ of Latter-day Saints, 1830–1898," 71.

Courtesy of the Church History Library, The Church of Jesus Christ of Latter-day Saints.

LESSON 6
Men and Women Are Stronger Together in the Lord's Work

Eliza R. Snow, who was serving as Relief Society general president at the time, understood the power that comes when men and women cooperate in the work of salvation. She traveled to Palestine as part of the company present at the rededication of the Holy Land in 1872. At age sixty-nine, she was the oldest in the company, but that didn't slow her down.

FOLLOWING HER BAPTISM IN 1835, Eliza R. Snow had witnessed important events in the history of the Church. She was baptized just five years after the Church's organization, and she was personally acquainted with the Prophet Joseph Smith. When Joseph organized the Female Relief Society of Nauvoo in 1842, Eliza was appointed secretary, and she carefully recorded the proceedings of those early meetings. Those minutes later became the organization's constitution and remain a valuable record for its affairs today.

Eliza arrived in the Salt Lake Valley in October 1847, just a few months after the first arriving wagons.[80] Later, in 1866, President Brigham Young called her to be president of the Relief Society, which

---

80 See Davidson, Karen Lynn and Jill Mulvay Derr, *Eliza: The Life and Faith of Eliza R. Snow* (Salt Lake City, UT: Deseret Book Company, 2013), ix.

had been largely dormant for nearly twenty years since the Saints' migration to Salt Lake. In this calling, Eliza oversaw the organization of ward Relief Societies and helped establish the first YWMIA and Primary organizations. She also helped introduce principles of welfare to the Church during her time as president, and responsibility for the welfare program remained largely in the Relief Society's hands during her service.

But despite all her leadership, Eliza was perhaps regarded more notably for her skill as a writer. The *Woman's Exponent*, a magazine for Relief Society sisters, was first published during her time as president. Additionally, she penned more than five hundred poems during her lifetime, many of which became the text for LDS hymns.[81] Her prolific writing earned her the nickname Zion's Poetess.

Saint. Secretary. Pioneer. President. Poet. Eliza's titles were many by 1872. But until then, she had never been called a missionary.

When President Brigham Young set Eliza apart for a mission to Palestine on October 14, 1872, it was the fulfillment of a prophecy the Prophet Joseph Smith had made decades prior. "You will yet visit Jerusalem," he had said to her.[82] Eliza made a record of the event:

> I recorded the saying in my Journal at the time, but had not reviewed it for many years, and the, to me, strange prediction had entirely gone from my memory—even when invited to join the Tourist party, although the anticipation of standing on the sacredly celebrated Mount of Olives inspired me with a feeling no language can describe; Joseph Smith's prediction did not occur to me until within a very few days of the time set for starting, when a friend brought it to my recollection, and

---

81 Ibid., viii.

82 Snow, Eliza R., "Sketch," in, *The Personal Writings of Eliza Roxcy Snow (Life Writings Frontier Women)*, edited by Maureen Ursenbach Beecher [1995], Vol. 1, 38.

then by reference to the long neglected Journal, the proof was before us. While on the tour, the knowledge of that predication inspired me with strength and fortitude.[83]

The tourist party was a group of Church leaders made up of mostly males, with the exception of Eliza Snow and Clara Little. Clara was a daughter of one of the men in the party and became Eliza's roommate during much of the journey.[84] President George A. Smith, first counselor to President Brigham Young, led the group.

"Tourist party" was a fitting designation. On their way to the Holy Land, the group did some sightseeing and visited Church members living in Europe. It was all part of the delegation's two-part commission to "see what opportunities there might be for preaching the gospel and to rededicate the Holy Land preparatory to the return of the Jews." Orson Hyde had previously traveled to the Holy Land and dedicated it for this purpose in 1840–1841, but he had done so alone. Now Church leaders "felt it was time to reassert the great interest the Church had in a regathering of the Jews to Palestine while the Saints were gathering to a new Zion in the West."[85]

Under these circumstances, Eliza's mission was unique among female missionaries of the time. As Church leaders observed conditions in Europe, learning where the gospel could be brought in the future, Eliza's viewpoints and understanding were vital. She understood then what we must understand now: The strengths of both men and women are necessary for the progress of the Church. The prophet called Eliza to serve alongside the brethren, just as today's prophet has called sister missionaries to serve alongside elders.

---

83 Ibid., 39.

84 See *Eliza: The Life and Faith of Eliza R. Snow*, 127–131.

85 "Brigham Young's Presidency: The Final Decade," in *Church History in the Fulness of Times*, chapter 32 [student manual 2003]; https:// www.lds.org/manual/church-history-in-the-fulness-of-times-student-manual/chapter-thirty-two-brigham-youngs-presidencythe-final-decade?lang=eng#16–32502_000_032; accessed Dec. 29, 2015.

One for the Ages

Sixty-nine-year-old Eliza R. Snow was among the oldest of the missionaries of the time, perhaps because the difficulty of travel made foreign missionary work impractical for many of the older generation. In other areas around the world, women still in their teens were accompanying their husbands on missions.

The appropriate age for missionary service has continued to vary since the Church's earliest missionary efforts. In 1951, women were eligible for missionary service at age twenty-three (see McKay, David O., Conference Report, April 1951, 81). *The minimum age for sisters was changed to twenty-one in 1960* (see Britsch, R. Lanier, "By All Means: The Boldness of the Mormon Missionary Enterprise," in *Go Ye into All the World: The Growth & Development of Mormon Missionary Work*, ed. Reid L. Nielson and Fred E. Woods [Provo, UT: Religious Studies Center, 2012], 1–20). *In 2012, the minimum age for sisters dropped from twenty-one to nineteen.*

And Eliza's advanced age didn't slow her down, as Elder Orson F. Whitney wrote after their return: "It was Sunday, March 2, 1873, when they ascended the Mount of Olives and held services, dedicating the land for the return of the Jews, this being the main purpose of their mission. They then completed the tour of the Holy Land, occupying in all about a month, during which 'Sister Eliza,' then in her seventieth year, slept in a tent, rode donkey-back, and endured the journey quite as well as the youngest and most vigorous of her fellow tourists."[86]

Eliza did not distinguish herself much from the men she served alongside, using pronouns like *we* and *us* in her descriptions of the trip. To her, it seemed, their differences were far less important than their commonalities in the service of God. In her record of the re-dedication of the Holy Land, she expressed feelings of reverence and humility for the work:

---

86 Whitney, Orson F., *History of Utah* (Oct. 1904), Vol. 1, 575.

After an opening prayer by Brother Carrington, we united in service in the order of the Holy Priesthood, President Smith leading in humble, fervent supplication, dedicating the land of Palestine for the gathering of the Jews and the rebuilding of Jerusalem, and returning heartfelt thanks and gratitude to God for the fulness of the Gospel and the blessings bestowed on the Latter-day Saints. Other brethren led in turn, and we had a very interesting season; to me it seemed the crowning point of the whole tour, realizing as I did that we were worshipping on the summit of the sacred Mount, once the frequent resort of the Prince of Life.[87]

Two dedicatory prayers were offered on the Mount of Olives that day—one by President Smith and the other by Elder Lorenzo Snow.[88] The fulfillment of these blessings is yet to come.

Today, the Church's proselyting efforts in the Holy Land are limited. The Church is not permitted to teach the gospel or perform baptisms in Israel, but just over two hundred Church members who joined the Church prior to living in Israel currently reside in the country. They worship in four congregations.[89]

As Eliza demonstrated, men and women in the Church today can draw strength from each other as they serve the Lord together with purpose and vitality.

---

87 Letter to the Editor of *Woman's Exponent* (Mar. 9, 1873), published in George A. Smith et al., *Correspondence of Palestine Tourists*, 260.

88 See Roberts, B. H., *A Comprehensive History of The Church of Jesus Christ of Latter-day Saints, Century One*, 6 vols. (Salt Lake City: The Church of Jesus Christ of Latter-day Saints, 1930), 5:474–75.

89 See Mormon Newsroom, Facts and Statistics, "Israel"; http://www. mormonnewsroom.org/facts-and-statistics/country/israel; accessed Dec. 29, 2015.

ZINA D. H. YOUNG

Courtesy of the Church History Library, The Church of Jesus Christ of Latter-day Saints.

LESSON 7
Make Everything You Do a Missionary Effort

Zina D. H. Young, who later succeeded Eliza R. Snow as Relief Society general president, left for New York in 1881 to gather family history records. Though not officially set apart as a missionary, she was counseled to take opportunities to speak as they presented themselves. Her experience is an inspiring example of how we can make any experience a missionary endeavor.

ZINA D. H. YOUNG WAS once told that a certain person disliked her. In response, she "looked quietly into the eyes of her informer and said, with simple dignity and sincerity: 'Well, I love her, Sister, and she can't help herself.'"[90]

If Eliza R. Snow was the head of women's work in Utah, Zina D. H. Young was the heart. At least, that was what Susa Young Gates said in the *History of the Young Ladies' Mutual Improvement Association:*

"Zina D. H. Young was the anti-type to Sister Snow. Some spoke of the two as the head and the heart of the women's work in Utah. Sister Snow was keenly intellectual, and she led by force of

90 Gates, Susa Young, *History of the Young Ladies' Mutual Improvement Association*, 1911, 22; http://contentdm.lib.byu.edu/cdm/ref/collection/NCMP1820-1846/id/27105; accessed November 30, 2016.

that intelligence. Sister Zina was all love and sympathy, and drew people after her by reason of that tenderness. It is well to consider them together in this work, for so they labored in Mutual Improvement side by side."[91]

Zina's tenderness and compassion came in the wake of challenges. Like many pioneer women, Zina experienced great loss. Her mother died when the Saints were driven from Missouri. Later, her father died when the Saints were forced to leave Nauvoo. She was pregnant when she finally headed west, and she gave birth in a wagon on the journey to Salt Lake.[92] She wrote in her journal, "Camped on Shugar Creek and here we found many dear ones, some comfortably fixed up . . . and others too sad to relate were it not that we knew it to be the work of God we were engaged in and He would bring us off victorious through all our hardships and toils."[93]

Zina knew The Church of Jesus Christ of Latter-day Saints was the Lord's true church, and she was committed to dedicating her life to its progression. She traveled extensively with Eliza R. Snow to organize Relief Societies, Young Women's Mutual Improvement Associations (precursors to today's Young Women organization), and Primaries throughout Utah. And on one occasion, she was set apart not as an official missionary but to "speak upon the principles of [her] faith as opportunity might be afforded"[94] while gathering family records in New York.

Zina was one of many women who was set apart to do this type of missionary work. These missionaries' primary concern was not with saving the living but with redeeming the dead.

---

91 Ibid., 21.

92 See "Zina Diantha Huntington Young: Third General President of the Relief Society, 1888–1901. https://www.lds.org/callings/relief-society/relief-society-presidents/zina-h-young?lang=eng; accessed Nov. 30, 2016.

93 Diary of Zina D. H. Young, 13. Quoted in "Great-Grandmother Zina: A More Personal Portrait," *Ensign*, March 1984; https://www.lds.org/ensign/1984/03/great-grandmother-zina-a-more-personal-portrait?lang=eng; accessed Nov. 30, 2016.

94 Whitney, Orson F., *History of Utah*, [Oct. 1904], Vol. 4, 577.

President Spencer W. Kimball taught that the threefold mission of the Church was "To proclaim the gospel of the Lord Jesus Christ to every nation, kindred, tongue and people; To perfect the Saints by preparing them to receive the ordinances of the gospel and by instruction and discipline to gain exaltation; To redeem the dead by performing vicarious ordinances of the gospel for those who have lived on the earth."[95]

Though each of these commissions remains equally important today, along with the newer fourth commission to care for the poor and needy, current full-time missionaries are primarily concerned with the first. But for one decade in the Church's history, several female missionaries were principally concerned with the third commission. They were set apart before leaving Utah to gather genealogical records elsewhere.

Mostly because of these genealogical missionaries, "the period from 1890 to 1898 saw more women involved in missionary labors than at any other time in Church history."[96] In 1890, eleven of the thirteen women set apart for missionary work were involved in family history efforts. These eleven women went to England, Scotland, Canada, Indiana, and other states, some of them alone, some with their husbands. The next year, nine of the sixteen female missionaries set apart were genealogical missionaries. Eight more genealogical missionaries were set apart before 1897.[97]

Obviously, not all female missionaries in the early 1890s were set apart for family-history-related purposes. It seemed women could be set apart to be missionaries during this time for almost any reason, including studying at a university, visiting family, or meeting a husband

---

95 Kimball, Spencer W., "A Report of My Stewardship," in Conference Report, April 1981.

96 Kunz, Calvin S., "A History of Female Missionary Activity in The Church of Jesus Christ of Latter-day Saints, 1830–1898," (master's thesis, Brigham Young University, 1976), 51–52; http://scholarsarchive.byu.edu/cgi/viewcontent.cgi?article=5857&context=etd.

97 Ibid., 44–45.

returning from a business trip.[98] Sometimes they were set apart without the expectation of their doing any actual missionary work. But of these incidental reasons for women to be set apart as missionaries, genealogical research was the most common. Thirty-four women served as genealogical missionaries between 1881 and 1897.[99]

Zina D. H. Young, who later served as Relief Society general president, was one of the first of these genealogical missionaries. Her trip to New York didn't begin as a missionary effort. She apparently planned the journey to her place of birth so she could obtain family records. But like all great member missionaries, she anticipated potential opportunities to share the gospel. As she prepared to leave in 1881, the First Presidency set her apart.

Zina's testimony burned inside her and could not be contained. Throughout her travels, she sought opportunities both to speak and to hear the word of God. Though she was sometimes refused, she also experienced success. The trip that began as a family-history excursion ended as something akin to a speaking and information-gathering tour for the lady from Utah. Of Zina's tour, Orson F. Whitney wrote, "Mrs. Young was cordially received by her relatives, and she addressed by invitation Sabbath schools and temperance meetings. She assisted to organize a Relief Society in New York, and with her foster son visited West Point, returning home, March 7, 1882. At the great gathering of representative women at the Chicago World's Fair in 1893, she sat upon the platform as the representative of the women of Utah."[100]

Upon her return, Zina continued to serve—sometimes conspicuously, sometimes quietly, but always faithfully. Susa Young Gates wrote of Zina, "In no other line of work and effort was Aunt Zina better known and more appreciated than in her ministrations to the sick and dying in the household of faith. She was an angel

---

98 Ibid., 41, 45.

99 Ibid., 42.

100 Whitney, Orson F., *History of Utah*, [Oct. 1904], Vol. 4, 577.

of hope and faith to thousands and thousands of the Latter-day Saints."[101]

Like Zina and the other women who served missions concurrent with other duties, Church members today can find opportunities to share the gospel and conspicuously live their faith in every circumstance.

Other Good Reasons

Prior to 1898, many sister missionaries served for reasons not directly related to preaching the gospel. In fact, many women who were set apart as missionaries never intended to teach the gospel—at least not directly. Women were sometimes set apart to do missionary work while traveling for other reasons, including visiting friends and relatives, gathering family history records, escaping persecution for polygamy, obtaining higher education, and serving as companions to missionary husbands (List from "A History of Female Missionary Activity in The Church of Jesus Christ of Latter-day Saints, 1830–1898," 40–48).

101 Gates, Susa Young, *History of the Young Ladies' Mutual Improvement Association*, 1911, 25; http://contentdm.lib.byu.edu/cdm/ref/collection/NCMP1820-1846/id/27105; accessed Nov. 30, 2016.

KATHERINE LOVE PAXMAN

PH 9867_f0001_Katherine Paxman.jpg, courtesy of the Church History Library, The Church of Jesus Christ of Latter-day Saints

LESSON 8
Overcome Trials with Faith in God and in Yourself

Katherine Love Paxman was a twenty-five-year-old new mother when she joined her husband on a mission to New Zealand. Unaccustomed to the climate and unfamiliar with the diseases on the islands, both Katherine and her baby girl became desperately ill a few months after their arrival. When tragedy struck and Katherine faced the seemingly impossible task of continuing her mission while being overwhelmed with grief, she exercised great faith in the Savior and in herself by engaging in the work with her whole heart.

KATHERINE ANN LOVE PAXMAN KNEW joining her husband on a mission to New Zealand wouldn't be easy, but the tragedy that accompanied her decision to go was worse than anything she had imagined. She was grief-stricken. In another week, her baby would have been eighteen months old.

On that day, she wrote in her journal, "Oh Heaven how can I write it. I was hastily called to arise this morning at 6 a.m. as our dear precious one was passing away, and at 15 minutes past 6, she breathed her last, and I, oh Heavenly Father, help me, was left with empty arms and a broken heart."[102]

The baby girl, Sarah Jane Love Paxman, had been Katherine's one constant friend and companion since Sarah's birth in Utah on

---

102 "Grandmother Paxman's Diary," courtesy Katie McCue, journal entry for March 10, 1887, 25.

September 17, 1885, because Katherine's husband, William, was frequently away from home. Katherine was understanding of his absence, but she missed his company.

When the baby was born, Katherine recorded her feelings with brevity and love: "Gave birth to a little daughter at 4 p.m. Weighed 10 lbs, weather bright, warm and sunshiny."[103]

The baby was nearly five months old when Katherine's mission call came. She learned about it when William wrote to her on February 15, 1886. He mentioned "an appointment that he had received to go to New Zealand and preside over that mission"[104] and asked Katherine to prepare to go to New Zealand with him. Katherine would be William's companion, but she ultimately spent more time with baby Sarah, as William's assignment as mission president frequently took him away.

Katherine knew little about the country she would soon call home. She didn't know missionaries from The Church of Jesus Christ of Latter-day Saints had first arrived in New Zealand in 1854, shortly after the Saints' arrival and settlement in Salt Lake. She didn't know that the country's population could essentially be divided into two groups—those of European descent and those native to the islands. She knew little of the distinct culture and language of the indigenous Maori people among whom she would soon be living. But her story and theirs would soon be indelibly intertwined.

The Lord was preparing the Maori people to hear the message of the restored gospel long before the missionaries arrived. Maori prophecies of the one true Church arriving in New Zealand seemed mythological at times, but scholarly accounts indicate that at least five different Maori priests accurately predicted the coming of the gospel. Many Maoris genuinely believed in these prophecies and their fulfillment.[105]

---

103 Ibid., September 17, 1885, 3.

104 Ibid., February 15, 1886, 3.

105 See "New Zealand, the Church in," in Ludlow, Daniel H., *Encyclopedia of Mormonism* (1992); http://eom.byu.edu/index.php/New_Zealand,_ the_Church_in; accessed Nov. 19, 2016.

In March of 1881, only a few years before Katherine, William, and their baby arrived in New Zealand, a certain Maori tribe held a gathering with representative natives to discuss the religious, political, and social issues affecting the Maori people. The conversation soon turned exclusively to religion. Most of those in attendance strongly believed in one of the Christian religions that had come to them. As the speakers recounted the history of Christianity in New Zealand, they began to wonder why there were so many different religions. If all the churches were founded on the teachings of Christ, they wondered, why wasn't there one church that had all the truth?[106]

They took this and other questions to Paora Potangaroa, who was well respected and was considered the "wisest chief and most learned sage among them."[107] After fasting, praying, and meditating for three days, he emerged with an answer: "My friends, the church for the Maori people has not yet come among us," he said. "You will recognize it when it comes. Its missionaries will travel in pairs. They will come from the rising sun. They will visit with us in our homes. They will learn our language and teach us the gospel in our own tongue. When they pray they will raise their right hands."[108] When missionaries from The Church of Jesus Christ of Latter-day Saints arrived seven months later, the Maori people recognized the Church as the one the sage had described.

Katherine and William were part of the fulfillment of that prophecy. When they arrived, headquarters for the Australasian Mission (also known as the Australian Mission) had moved from Sydney, Australia, to Auckland, New Zealand. Missionaries routinely learned Maori and taught the native people in their own language. They lived with the Maoris and adapted to their culture.

---

106 See Cowley, Matthew, "Maori Chief Predicts," *Te Karere*, Nov. 1950. Quoted in Deseret Book Company, *Matthew Cowley Speaks*, 201.

107 Ibid.

108 Cowley, Matthew, "Maori Chief Predicts," *Te Karere*, November 1950. Quoted in *Matthew Cowley Speaks* (Salt Lake City, UT: Deseret Book Company, 200–05).

But living so close to the Maoris, with no immunity to their diseases, took its toll on both Katherine and her little girl. In February 1887, both became ill. On February 21, Katherine wrote in her journal, "I have been very sick, also Baby. I was confined to my bed for three weeks and for one week could not look after Baby at all, so one of the native sisters took her and would keep her all night and then wash and dress her in the morning for me, then I would manage to see to her the rest of the day. . . . If dear Sarah had not been sick too, it would not have been quite so hard, but oh, how my heart strings have been wrung."[109]

Katherine got better, but Sarah got worse. Whatever disease had ailed Katherine had certainly infected her child as well, but complications wreaked havoc in the girl's tiny body. She soon seemed to be suffering from whooping cough and had a heavy fever. She was also teething, which left her in additional pain and gave her a canker. The Paxmans had the baby "anointed and administered to, two or three times every day," but the little relief these blessings brought never lasted long.[110]

The day before the baby died, Katherine wrote her feelings in her journal. "Yesterday we all fasted again and then dedicated her to God our Father, but still pleaded for her restoration to health if it is his will but we say 'Thy will, O Father, not ours.' Oh Father, strengthen and sustain us, our hearts are breaking, but oh, I know full well that if it is Father's will, she can still be healed and raised in health to us. God grant that it may be so."[111]

The baby slept peacefully that night. Then the morning came, and the baby's life was over. William wrote: "Our lovely little girl gradually became weaker and weaker, day by day. We did everything that layed in our power for her recovery . . . it was hard for us to

---

109 *Katherine Ann Humphrey Love Paxman (my Grandmother)* (February 21, 1887), 22.

110 Ibid., March 1, 1887, 24.

111 Ibid., March 9, 1887, 25.

believe that the Lord required us to lay her body down in this far off land, but we were forced to this conclusion."[112]

Now Katherine knelt by her daughter's grave thousands of miles from her home. Swallowed up by grief, both Katherine and her husband knew they had a choice to make. They could become bitter and angry at the sacrifice required of them, or they could accept the tragedy as the will of God, serve Him, and have faith that they would one day be reunited with their baby. To their eternal credit, they chose the latter.[113]

William wrote, "When we look to the bright future we feel comforted. We know she is still our sweet jewel and will be forever."[114]

In her journal, Katherine wrote, "She slept and rested so peacefully all night and passed away so peacefully, but oh how my poor heart is lacerated and bleeding over my bereavement. . . . She looked so nice, as her sweet little face was no longer drawn and contorted with pain. Oh my dear sweet angel child how can I stand it to have your dear little body laid away in this far away land. God alone can sustain me in this hour of affliction."[115]

Given time to grieve, Katherine reflected on what she must do for the remainder of her mission and, indeed, her life. "We left the grave with broken hearts and empty arms, oh God grant that I may be faithful in all things, and that my deep affliction may be sanctified

---

112 See Kunz, Calvin S., "A History of Female Missionary Activity in The Church of Jesus Christ of Latter-day Saints, 1830–1898," (master's thesis, Brigham Young University, 1976), 77; http://scholarsarchive.byu.edu/cgi/viewcontent.cgi?article=5857&context=etd.

113 Ibid., 77.

114 Paxman, James W., "William Paxman: 1835–1897, A Brief Biographical Sketch," (1937), 17.

115 *Katherine Ann Humphrey Love Paxman (my Grandmother)*, March 10, 1887, 25.

"A Sad and Tragic Event"

The first sister missionary to die in the mission field was Sister Katie Eliza Hale Merrill, who died in Samoa at age nineteen of complications after childbirth. The Deseret Evening News *reported her death this way:*

> *We have very bad news to report this month, and our hearts are filled with sympathy for all those who will be affected by the same. In reporting Sister Merrill's condition last month we thought she was recovering but she had a billious attack and could not keep any food on her stomach. As a result she became very weak and a premature birth was the consequence. This happened on the 28th of June. The child died next day. An hour after the death of the child, the mother called Sister Lee to her bedside and after thanking her for waiting on her during her sickness, said that she was 'going to die,' that she 'could not stay' because 'they had come for her.' She then talked with her husband, kissed him goodbye, and all was over. This sad event has left a cloud of sorrow behind that nothing but time and the Spirit of God can dispel.* ("She Passed Away While on a Mission to Samoa," *Deseret Evening News*, Aug. 11, 1891, 6, Church Archives.)

Katie and her baby were buried in the same coffin 200 yards from the mission house. Her heartbroken husband wrote, "Katie slept well last night. . . . At 1 o'clock I witnessed the death of our baby. And at 3 o'clock p.m. God saw fit to take my dear wife. It is all I can bare. We left home so happy . . . and now I am left alone . . . bereft of all my earthly joys. . . . Unless I can overcome the sorrow and trials that are now heaped upon me I am crushed" (Quoted in Kunz, Calvin S., "A History of Female Missionary Activity in The Church of Jesus Christ of Latter-day Saints, 1830–1898," (master's thesis, Brigham Young University, 1976), 77–78; http://scholarsarchive.byu.edu/cgi/viewcontent.cgi?article=5857&context=etd).

unto me, and that I may be worthy of meeting and dwelling eternally with my darling."[116]

Perhaps the grieving mother was able to move forward at least partially because of the work she and her husband were assigned not long after they buried the baby. In addition to her duties in the mission home, she was now assigned to work alongside her husband in a cause that would bless the people of New Zealand for years to come: the translation of the Book of Mormon into the Maori language.[117]

As president of the mission, William presided over the work. Two New Zealand missionaries, Ezra F. Richards and Sonda Sanders, began translating the Book of Mormon into Maori in 1887 with assistance from some native Maoris. Katherine was assigned to transcribe the missionaries' translations in longhand, an incredibly time-consuming task that she undertook while keeping house in the mission home, cooking for the missionaries, and seeing to other practical needs.[118] Katherine noted in her journal a few days after Elder Richards and Elder Sanders began translating that she "commenced copying the manuscript of the Book of Mormon translated in Maori"—but only "after breakfast and morning work [was] done."[119]

Seven months later, the translation was complete. Of the night she finished, she wrote, "Just as I called the brethren to supper, they announced that they had completed the last page of the book. In the evening, they translated the testimonies of the witnesses thus completing the translation of the Book of Mormon into the Maori language at 17 minutes to nine o'clock on the evening of November 24, 1887 at Rakaikiteroa."[120]

---

116 Ibid., March 11, 1887, 26.

117 See Kunz, Calvin S., "A History of Female Missionary Activity in The Church of Jesus Christ of Latter-day Saints, 1830–1898," (master's thesis, Brigham Young University, 1976), 64; http://scholarsarchive.byu.edu/cgi/viewcontent.cgi?article=5857&context=etd.

118 See Oler, Katherine Paxman, "Biography of Katherine Ann Humphrey Love Paxman," 2.

119 *Katherine Ann Humphrey Love Paxman (my Grandmother)*, April 30, 1887.

120 Ibid., November 24, 1887.

A year later, the Book of Mormon in Maori was almost ready for publication. Katherine was ready to go home, as she was expecting another baby. She bid a tender farewell to her husband and her Maori friends late in 1888. Though Katherine wasn't present when the Maori people received their first copies of the book, William's record of their reaction was proof that the Lord could use even a broken, grieving heart to help accomplish His work.

William reported: "One of the leading features of our recent conference and one that gave great joy unto the saints was having 500 copies of the Book of Mormon in Maori to distribute among them. Never were children more anxious to receive their Christmas gifts than were this people to receive that holy book."[121]

Katherine's contribution is not mentioned in most accounts of its translation, but she labored diligently through her grief. She completed her mission with faith in the Lord and faith in the future. In so doing, she brought joy not only to herself but also to the Maori people who would now read the Book of Mormon in their language. Like Katherine, missionaries today can overcome trials and succeed in God's work with faith in the Lord.

---

121 Quoted in "Wiliam Paxman: 1835–1897, A Brief Biographical Sketch," 21.

ELIZABETH "LIBBIE" NOALL

LESSON 9
Learn All You Can, Do All You Can

Elizabeth "Libbie" Noall was a newlywed of five months when she and her new husband arrived in the Sandwich Islands in 1885. She was twenty years old; her husband was twenty-two. Despite her youth and relative inexperience, she became fluent in the native language and was instrumental in building up the Church on the islands, even while bearing and raising young children.

President Joseph F. Smith waited for his breakfast while Libbie Noall worked in the kitchen. She was serving as a missionary alongside her husband, Matthew, in the Hawaiian Mission. She shared in many of Matthew's responsibilities and, later that week, would preside at the Relief Society meetings held as part of the mission conference President Smith was planning to attend.[122] But for now, she was cooking breakfast.

Or, at least, she was trying. Apparently, the woman who was supposed to have done the grocery shopping had not purchased enough

---

122 See Fisher, George H., "Hawaiian Mission Conference," *The Deseret Weekly*, May 11, 1895, 659.

food for the small crowd gathered in their home. They had some food but not nearly enough. Libbie would have to make do with what she had on hand, which, she realized as she gazed around the kitchen, amounted to some dishes, a handful of mush, and a few old dishrags.

Suddenly, it came to her. An almost imperceptible smile came to her face as she envisioned her plan. Mathew noticed her expression and gave her a questioning look.

"You'll see," she said, thinking through her plan and rolling up her sleeves.

A moment later, Libbie entered the dining room with a dish brimming over with food, hot and delicious-looking. She placed it before President Smith, who looked pleased.

"It Was Always a Joy"

Julina Smith was one of many LDS women who studied obstetrics and became a midwife. Many of them considered this both a job and a sacred calling.

Of her work with mothers and babies, Julina wrote, "When the mother of three children, I studied Obstetrics and Nursing under the best physicians in Utah, and the knowledge acquired stood me in good stead not only in our own family but in hundreds of cases where I have responded to calls from expectant mothers. And it was always a joy for me to place a tiny one for the first time in its mother's arms, for I felt again the thrills that I felt on looking in to my own babies' faces" (Newton, Honey M., "Zion's Hope: Pioneer Midwives and Women Doctors in Utah" [2013], 65).

She returned to the kitchen three times, each time returning with a serving dish piled high with mush. She placed each dish along the middle of the table and took her seat.

One of the elders reached forward with a spoon just as President Smith dipped a spoon into his food. Both men stopped short, their utensils halting just below the surface of the mush.

President Smith laughed as the secret to Libbie's means of providing food became apparent. The other man who had begun to eat looked resentful as he pulled out his spoon and used it to push the mush aside. Just below each thin layer of food lay a large, crumpled, old dishrag.[123]

A few guests laughed quietly, and Libbie joined them.

Their laughter spread as the angry man stood and spoke over the sound. "This is a clever April fool breakfast," he shouted. "I accept it at face value." The laughter continued as a few men stood and joined the angry one. They left the house to find a proper breakfast of oysters and other luxurious foods at a nearby restaurant.[124]

Libbie could laugh when things didn't go as expected, but her depth of character and dedication to missionary work ran deep.

The night they arrived, the Noalls found their lodging, which was only a small room in disrepair. It had a seven-foot-high ceiling with cloth loosely dangling from it, probably put there some time ago to cover holes in the roof. The wind came through gaping holes in the walls, blowing the cloth pathetically as it hung like a partition between the room's two beds. Large pieces of the floor had been broken away, and rats scurried above and below the Noalls as they prepared for sleep. [125] Matthew Noall wrote later:

> All night long the rats played hide and go seek along the ceiling joists and up and down the curtain. One or two of them stopped long enough, however, to tear part of the leather lining from a pair of shoes which I had asked Brother Solomon in Salt Lake City to make especially durable for my long sojourn away from home. On our side of the curtain [Matthew's

---

123 See Noall, Matthew, "To My Children: An Autobiographical Sketch" (1947), 36–37, Church Archives.

124 Ibid., 37.

125 Ibid., 31–32.

comical name for the cloth that hung from the ceiling] Libbie, who was only twenty years old, chose the inside of the bed because she thought that she would be safe there from the rats; but they played up and down beside her all night long.[126]

Some time later, the Noalls accepted an assignment to build new missionary housing. Libbie made the curtains, drapes, and valances.[127]

Sewing drapes was the type of practical, necessary work the Church needed missionary wives to do, especially in underdeveloped areas like the islands, and Libbie was a skilled seamstress. Many of the wives she served with considered such tasks their primary obligation, and while this may have been the case for Libbie as well, she expanded her influence to bless as many people in Hawaii as she could.

First, she had to learn the native Hawaiian language. Her husband noted later how unusual it was for a missionary—and especially a female one—to learn the Hawaiian language so well:

> I think I am safe in saying that up to this time . . . not more than one-third of the men missionaries on the Islands had ever learned the language sufficiently well to carry on a conversation at all fluently with the natives. And among the wives of the missionaries—though the women were supposed to labor among the natives as gospel teachers—there were only two who succeeded in learning it well enough to converse readily in the Hawaiian tongue. These two women were a Sister Cluff, wife

---

126 Ibid., 32–33.

127 See "A History of Female Missionary Activity in The Church of Jesus Christ of Latter-day Saints, 1830–1898," 83.

of the mission president, and my own wife Libbie. They moved among the native women with great freedom, and were a source of comfort and inspiration to them.

It was Matthew's impression that many women didn't learn the language "due . . . to the preconceived idea that they were not there as missionary-teachers but as wives."[128]

Libbie was called as president of the Relief Society in the Hawaiian Mission. She helped establish the children's Primary organization in both Honolulu and Laie and anointed and gave blessings to women in confinement, just as Louisa Barnes Pratt had done.[129]

In this calling, Libbie also traveled from one side of Honolulu to the other, entering the homes of native families to teach lessons in religion and in household management.[130] Getting to these appointments was a struggle. No trolleys had been built in the city yet, and hiring a carriage was an expense the mission couldn't easily afford. Sometimes she took a horse, but after her first child, Vera, was born, getting around on horseback became almost impossible. To solve the problem, Libbie hired a Hawaiian girl to tend Vera while she made visits. She was away when Vera took her first steps, but Matthew was caring for Vera that day, so he was there to see it.[131]

Giving birth on the islands had been an ordeal. Three thousand miles from home, the first-time mother had no family nearby to assist in the labor. Fortunately, Julina Smith, wife of Joseph F. Smith, was in Hawaii and assisted in the labor. She was a midwife

---

128 Noall, Matthew, "To My Children: An Autobiographical Sketch" (1947), 27–28, Church Archives.

129 See Kunz, Calvin S., "A History of Female Missionary Activity in The Church of Jesus Christ of Latter-day Saints, 1830–1898," (master's thesis, Brigham Young University, 1976), 64; http://scholarsarchive.byu.edu/cgi/viewcontent.cgi?article=5857&context=etd.

130 Ibid., 46.

131 Noall, Matthew, "To My Children: An Autobiographical Sketch" (1947), 46–47, Church Archives.

and had delivered her own son with just the help of her husband eleven days before Vera's birth. Julina delivered two babies that day.[132]

Libbie ultimately spent several years in Hawaii, and in those years, she acted as a midwife herself on several occasions. She had her second child, Nora, during their first mission to Hawaii and her fourth child, George, during their second.

Between the Noalls' two missions, Libbie served in Hawaii for a total of seven years and five months. She died at age thirty-two after failure to recover sufficiently from childbirth.[133] That was in 1897, the year before the first full-time, single, certified, set-apart sister missionaries were called to serve in England.

Her obituary paid tribute to her missions, recognizing that she learned and did everything she could to expand her sphere of influence. "[In Hawaii] her native ability [for speaking and writing] made itself manifest in the rapid manner in which she acquired the Hawaiian language. . . . It is doubtful if any white woman not born or raised on the Islands ever spoke the language more fluently than did Sister Noall. She is known and respected in every village and hamlet on the islands where any Latter-day Saints reside, and many a heart-felt tear will be shed when the sad news of her death reaches the field of her devoted labors."[134]

Libbie Noall magnified her calling as a missionary by doing all that was required of her and then a little more. She was not expected to learn the Hawaiian language, but because she did, she could testify of Christ to many more people on her mission. Like Libbie, missionaries today can magnify their influence as they learn and do all they can.

---

132 Ibid., 49.

133 Ibid., 107.

134 "Utah News," *The Latter-Day Saints' Millennial Star*, April 15, 1897, Vol. 59, No. 15, 239.

ELIZABETH CLARIDGE McCUNE

Used by permission, Utah State Historical Society.

LESSON 10
Women Have a Unique Convincing Ability

Elizabeth Claridge McCune teaches us that a missionary force consisting only of men lacks a valuable advantage. Elizabeth softened hearts by publicly addressing crowds of hostile people and, in doing so, demonstrated that women have a unique convincing ability. Her missionary service in England in 1897 and 1898 led mission leaders to request more lady missionaries like her.

ELIZABETH CLARIDGE MCCUNE, WHO WAS born in England but raised in Nephi, Utah, now lived in London. The Mormon woman wanted to help the young men serving as missionaries in England, and she determined to do everything she could to do so. But she couldn't have imagined the effect her efforts would have on future generations of young women in the Church.

Elizabeth grew up in the Church and married her childhood sweetheart, Alfred W. McCune. His business success provided the McCunes with a comfortable living and the means to travel, so they began an extensive tour of Europe in February 1897 when Elizabeth was forty-five years old. The trip took them to England, France, and Italy and included a visit to their missionary son in Great Britain. While they regarded this as a primarily sightseeing trip, Elizabeth hoped to do some genealogical research as well.

In preparation for this spiritual aspect of the trip, Elizabeth sought a priesthood blessing before her departure. President Lorenzo Snow administered that blessing. She expected words of guidance regarding her family history, but his words suggested a different purpose for the trip: "Thy mind shall be as clear as an angel's when explaining the principles of the Gospel."[135]

Upon their arrival in England, Elizabeth and her children remained in London for some time. They provided the missionaries with a place to live and assisted in their labors. Elizabeth often held the elders' hats and coats while they preached in the streets, and she helped them distribute tracts from door to door.

Still, she yearned to do more. "While abroad I always had a burning desire in my heart to give our Father's children what I knew to be the Truth. Wherever I went to visit and had an opportunity to converse with the people I would lead up to this the uppermost topic in my mind. Often I had the privilege of proclaiming the Gospel to people who had never before heard of it. I asked myself, at times, 'Why do I feel so, I am not a missionary?' I told my daughter one day that I believed the time was not far distant when women would be called on missions. I often felt if I were commissioned of God as the young men were, I could have gone into every house and entered into a quiet religious chat with the people; leaving with each one my earnest testimony. It was a constant surprise to me to find so many people who had never heard of our Gospel. The people of England are a good and an honest people and I longed to see them partaking of the blessings of the true Gospel of Christ."[136]

One day, Elizabeth, who was on her way to the Queen's Jubilee with her daughter, noticed that the elders at Hyde Park were singing a hymn with the hope of attracting a crowd for an "open air" meeting.

---

135 Gates, Susa Young, "Biographical Sketches: Mrs. Elizabeth Claridge McCune," Young Woman's Journal, Vol. 9, No. 8, August 1898, 339.

136 Ibid., 339–340.

Eager to assist the missionaries, Elizabeth and her daughter rushed to join them.

"We hurried across and joined in the dear old hymn with considerable vigor and telling effect. The people came flocking around us from all directions. I was congratulating myself and the others on the brilliant effect of our music, when a fashionably-dressed dude came up."

The man, however, hadn't come because of their superior singing. In an English accent, he said, "Oh, dear! Oh, dear! What a horrible noise they do make in our park—to be sure!"[137]

Elizabeth's memory of the unimpressed Londoner in the park was amusing, but the rumors circulating in the area about Mormons were not. Notably, a book William Jarman, a former Church member, wrote was creating a public relations nightmare for the Church. His book, *U.S.A.: Uncle Sam's Abscess, or Hell Upon Earth,*[138] presented Mormons as a misguided people, describing their beliefs as a religion "where polygamy, incest, and murder are taught and practised as religion under the 'all seeing eye,' and the sign 'holiness unto the Lord'"[139]—and that was just on the title page.

The book's sensational claims and perceived legitimacy—it was written by a former Church member, after all—attracted a large readership in England. The book painted a particularly unflattering portrait of Mormon women and their lives in Utah. And with only male missionaries available to speak on behalf of the Church, missionary efforts were significantly impeded.

With these difficulties on their minds, British Mission President Rulon S. Wells and his counselor Joseph W. McMurrin prepared for the semiannual London conference at the end of 1897. Church

---

137 In the original text, the dialect is spelled out phonetically. See ibid., 341.

138 See Jarman, William, U.S.A.: *Uncle Sam's Abscess, or Hell upon Earth* (1884); https://archive.org/stream/usaunclesamsabs00jarmgoog#page/n5/mode/2up.

139 This text is from the book's title page, which can be found at the web address in endnote 149.

members living in and around London gathered at the Clerkenwall Town Hall to receive enlightenment and instruction, but people of other faiths were in attendance as well. Elizabeth McCune attended the afternoon session.

The "Utah Girl" Effect

Elizabeth McCune left England when there was still much to do, and her efforts inspired Church leaders to call more women to proselyte in England and dispel misconceptions about the Church. This led to many faithful women following in Elizabeth's wake, including Ann Dewey Campbell.

Sister Campbell was set apart for a mission in England in 1898. Once, during a street meeting, a vicar of the Church of England asked Sister Campbell if the missionaries were Mormons, to which she replied, "Yes, sir."

The incident was reported in the Deseret Evening News*:*

The reverend could scarcely be persuaded to hold his peace till Brother Parkin finished speaking. As soon as the "amen" was spoken, [the vicar] said, "These people are liars and deceivers; they don't tell the truth about their religion. Their Elders come here to carry off girls and women to Utah. They are murderers and cut-throats. Their women are low, depraved and down trodden. They are followers of Brigham Young, who had sixty wives," etc.

He spoke for twenty minutes in this manner.

At the first opportunity Brother Parkin introduced our Utah girl to the crowd of nearly two hundred. Sister Campbell stepped forward and in a loud, clear voice, told of the virtue and morality of the women and men of Utah. In concluding she bore a powerful testimony to the Gospel of Jesus Christ. Much good was done and more prejudice erased by Sister Campbell's remarks and influence ("Missionary Work in England," *Deseret Evening News*, Sept. 17, 1889, 5, Church Archives.)

Elizabeth later said, "Brother Wells and Brother McMurrin spoke with great freedom and convincing force. It seemed to me the whole audience must be converted by the power manifested."

They weren't, though, at least not yet. Elizabeth's observation continued: "Then Brother McMurrin spoke of the base falsehoods which Jarman and his daughters had so industriously circulated regarding the Mormon women being confined behind a wall in Utah, and of their ignorance and degraded condition."

Then Brother McMurrin surprised everyone in attendance with his promise of a special guest speaker who would be addressing them later in the day: "We have with us just now, a lady from Utah who has traveled all over Europe with her husband and family, and hearing of our conference, she has met with us. We are going to ask Sister McCune to speak this evening and tell you of her experience in Utah."[140]

Elizabeth grew anxious as her impromptu address drew near. Brother McMurrin had invited everyone in attendance to bring others to listen to "the lady from Utah."

Of the announcement, she said, "This announcement nearly frightened me to death. But the Elders assured me that they would give me their faith and prayers, and I added my own fervent appeals to my Heavenly Father for aid and support. I said in my heart, 'O, if we only had one of our good woman speakers from Utah to take advantage of this grand opportunity what good she might do!"[141]

But deferring to someone she considered more qualified was not an option for Elizabeth. The opportunity to speak on behalf of the Mormon women in Utah to a full house of skeptics was hers alone.

The hall grew crowded as the time for the meeting approached. People brought in extra chairs to accommodate the growing crowd, and someone opened the gallery doors, but even then, people were

---

140 "Biographical Sketches, Elizabeth Claridge McCune," 342.

141 Ibid.

turned away for lack of space.[142] Elizabeth recorded what happened next:

> With a final prayer I arose to address the audience. I told them my father had heard and embraced the Gospel in England, and had left [his] father, mother, brothers and sisters, and with his wife and babies had emigrated to Utah, to unite with a people who knew God and were trying to keep His commandments. I told them I had been raised in Utah and knew almost every foot of the country and most of the people. I spoke of my extensive travels in America and in Europe, and said that nowhere had I found women held in such esteem as among the Mormons of Utah. Our husbands are proud of their wives and daughters; they do not consider that they were created solely to wash dishes and tend babies; but they give them every opportunity to attend meetings and lectures and to take up everything which will educate and develop them. Our religion teaches us that the wife stands shoulder to shoulder with the husband. If the Mormon women of Utah had to do half or quarter of the hard work that I see your women here in England doing, they would think themselves cruelly abused, and very few would submit to it. Many other things I told them. At the close of the meeting several strangers shook me by the hand and said, "If more of your women would come out here a great amount of good would be done." Another gentleman said, "I have always had a desire in my heart to see a Mormon woman

---

142 See Bruce, W. G., "London Conference," *The Latter-day Saints' Millennial Star*, Oct. 28, 1897, 684.

and to hear her speak. Madam, you carry truth in your voice and words."[143]

By the time Elizabeth left for Italy with her husband a short while later, she had spoken again at the Nottingham conference and had requests to speak at many more meetings. Though she could not stay, her success gave President McMurrin an idea.

He and other leaders wrote letters to the First Presidency shortly after Elizabeth's departure, "setting forth the work done by . . . sisters, who voluntarily without being specially called, had assisted in the mission field, further pointing out the grand possibilities, as regards the work to be accomplished, and old erroneous ideas rampant in the average mind to be removed, by setting apart sisters from Zion to fulfil missions."[144]

Elizabeth's desire to testify of Christ and her willingness to speak when called upon guided her missionary labors. At the time, her great missionary contribution was to help break down anti-Mormon propaganda about women that had prevented the missionaries' success in England. But the long-term effects of her mission are equally consequential. Largely because of her excellent work, Church leaders began calling upon the untapped missionary resource they had in the women of the Church. Elizabeth Claridge McCune helped pave the way for generations of sister missionaries who would serve after her.

---

143 "Biographical Sketches, Elizabeth Claridge McCune," 342–43.

144 G. E. C., "Our First Lady Missionaries," *The Latter-day Saints' Millennial Star*, Vol. 60, July 28, 1898, 472–73.

JENNIE BRIMHALL

Photo courtesy of D.V. Groberg family

LESSON 11
How Long We Serve Is Less Important
Than How Well We Serve

Jennie Brimhall secured for herself a permanent place in Church history as one of the first single sisters to be called as an official proselyting full-time missionary. But when health problems sent her home earlier than anticipated, she demonstrated that in the Church of Jesus Christ, the amount of time we serve in a calling isn't nearly as important as how well we serve.

THE LETTER PRESIDENT MCMURRIN WROTE to the First Presidency found its way to President Wilford Woodruff's desk, and the request for more sister missionaries was granted. After nearly seventy years of both official and unofficial missionary service by female members of The Church of Jesus Christ of Latter-day Saints, the first single, full-time proselyting sister missionaries were officially called and set apart in April 1898.

Lucy Jane "Jennie" Brimhall was twenty-three years old and had completed some courses at Brigham Young Academy in her native Provo, Utah. She and her childhood friend, Inez Knight, decided to take a trip to Europe to visit Inez's brothers and go sightseeing.[145]

---

145 See Lelegren, Kelly, *"Real, Live Mormon Women": Understanding the Role of Early Twentieth-Century LDS Lady Missionaries* (master's thesis, Utah State University, 2009), 23; digitalcommons.usu.edu/etd/415/.

As Jennie was planning her trip, Church leaders in Salt Lake City were making other plans. President George Q. Cannon articulated the First Presidency's desire to call sisters to serve as missionaries when he said, "There will be an opportunity, doubtless, for women who are capable and who desire to do good, to go out, under proper conditions; . . . They can do a great many things that would assist in the propagation of the Gospel of the Lord Jesus Christ."[146]

Jennie's planned vacation and the First Presidency's desire for female missionaries merged into a mission call. A brief conversation between Jennie and her bishop, followed by correspondence between local leaders and the First Presidency, resulted in the two women receiving calls to serve as missionaries in Great Britain. They were set apart on April 1, 1898.

Of that occasion, Jennie wrote, "I received word to be present at Brother Jesse Knight's home and there be set apart as a missionary to Great Britain. We were then set apart, . . . I was then given a certificate and am thus numbered among the full-fledged missionaries of the Church."[147]

Jennie arrived in Great Britain in the wake of women like Elizabeth McCune, who had already done much to share the gospel with people both curious about and hostile toward women from Utah.

Shortly after her arrival in England with Inez, though, Jennie experienced health problems. She returned home honorably in November after eight months in the mission field. While Jennie had an enriching and rewarding mission, its short duration allowed for fewer of the life-changing experiences other missionaries encountered.

Later in life, Inez wrote a tribute to Jennie in the *Relief Society Magazine*: "She visited with the presidency of the European mission, all the conferences . . . in England, Scotland and Wales. So effective

---

146 Cannon, George Q., in Conference Report, Apr. 1898, 8.

147 Kunz, Calvin S., "A History of Female Missionary Activity in The Church of Jesus Christ of Latter-day Saints, 1830–1898," (master's thesis, Brigham Young University, 1976), 37; http://scholarsarchive. byu.edu/cgi/viewcontent.cgi?article=5857&context=etd.

was her testimony that after twenty years an unbeliever who listened to her speak wrote, saying he could never forget her sincere, guileless expression and was led further to investigate and receive the blessings of membership. She filled an honorable mission, making many real friends."[148]

More important than her labors as a missionary was Jennie's dedication to the gospel after her full-time missionary service was over. She married Inez's brother Will Knight in January 1899—he completed his mission the same time she did—and the two of

For the Foreseeable Future

Because female missionaries were still new and no standard precedent had been set, many of the first sisters, including Jennie Brimhall, probably left for their missions without knowing when they might return. Some women, like Jennie, returned after just a few months. The standard length of missionary service for young women is now eighteen months, but that wasn't standardized until 1971 (See "'Our Wise and Prudent Women': Twentieth-Century Trends in Female Missionary Service," in *New Scholarship on Latter-day Saint Women in the Twentieth Century*, ed. Carol Cornwall Madsen and Cherry B. Silver (2005), 126–28).

them moved to Canada. Jennie served as president of their stake's MIA, and her husband served as a bishop. Their life in Canada was "typical of wholesome hospitality."[149]

Later, Will and Jennie returned with their children to Provo. Again, she served as president of her stake's MIA. In 1921, Jennie was called as first counselor to Clarissa S. Williams, general president of the Relief Society, and served for seven years.

Jennie may have made her initial mark on Church history by serving as one of the first official female missionaries, but she

---

148 Allen, Inez Knight, "Jennie Brimhall Knight" in *Relief Society Magazine*, December 1928, 646.

149 Ibid.

proved worth remembering forever by remaining true to her testimony and the gospel to the end. Jennie Brimhall proved that in the Lord's service, it's not where, when, or for how long you serve in official capacities. It's all about how you serve and how much you love the Lord as you do so.

AMANDA "INEZ" KNIGHT

LESSON 12
We Can Overcome Fear with Faith

Amanda "Inez" Knight was the first official single, full-time proselyting sister missionary in this dispensation, having been set apart just before her friend Jennie Brimhall. Though she encountered nerves and anxiety in her new calling, she faced them with courage and served honorably. Inez's experience teaches an important truth to Church members everywhere: we can overcome fear and believe in a bright future ahead.

WHEN AMANDA "INEZ" KNIGHT WAS called to serve as a full-time missionary in 1898, she joined two of her brothers in Great Britain. She and her close friend Jennie Brimhall were chosen in part because they were the type of women the Church wanted people in England to become acquainted with: they were educated and capable, mature and eloquent.

When Inez arrived in England, anti-Mormon sentiment was strong. One particular day after poor health forced Jennie to return to Utah and while Inez was serving with her companion Liza Chipman, the pair came across a group of people antagonistic toward the Church. These people declared that the Mormon elders had come to England to entice English women to come back to

Utah and be slaves to the men. "If they [do] not do as the men tell them, their throats [are] cut!" one of them said.[150]

This time, Inez and Liza held their peace until the encounter was over. But it was not the last time the women would have an opportunity to allay prejudice. And though she had great anxiety over the prospect, Inez eventually learned to respond to such confrontations with faith in the Lord.

Church leadership hoped that the presence of women like Inez, Jennie, and Liza would curtail the incorrect assumptions. While the presence of "real live Mormon women"[151] had changed many minds in the past and would continue to do so, the prevailing religious climate in England did not change quickly.

Inez understood at least some of the reasons she had been called to serve in England. Perhaps this was why she frequently expressed distress and anxiety when she wrote in her journal about speaking in public. After several entries mentioning her anxieties, Inez wrote: "Attended and spoke in street meeting. Regular cottage meeting we took part in. Still it seemed to me I was worse frightened every time I was called upon to talk. Oh those fearful trembling feelings I shall never forget, if I ever am free from them."[152]

In truth, she may have been right to be nervous. Not everyone in England liked what the Mormon women had to say. One night in January 1899, Inez and her companion Liza were on their way to visit the family who kept house at the local mission headquarters. Just outside the building, they encountered a large group of people waiting for them.

---

150 Maki, Elizabeth, "'Taking Fresh Courage': Antagonists Directed Attacks at First Sister Missionaries," May 4, 2012, Church Archives; http://history.lds.org/article/inez-knight-opposition?lang=eng; accessed Nov. 19, 2016.

151 Maki, Elizabeth, "'Real Live Mormon Women': Inez Knight Took on Weighty Role of Ambassador for LDS Women," July 2, 2012, Church Archives; http://history.lds.org/article/inez-knight-ambassador?lang=eng;

152 Inez Knight Allen diary, 1898–99, L. Tom Perry Special Collections, Harold B. Lee Library, Brigham Young University, Provo, Utah, 22.

Inez wrote: "As we went in they hissed & shouted at us, & after we were in rocks were thrown thick & fast in the windows until not a glass remained in the house. Ray [Inez's brother and fellow missionary] finally took us girls home, but the mob followed us & threw rocks & mud & sticks at us all the way to the police station. . . . We both cried but could not help it to think of being so treated in a civilized nation. The chief police went to our home with us."[153]

But there were good times too. Inez eventually overcame her fear of public speaking and saw great missionary success. In 1899, she reflected on her mission and wrote, "Many have been led to investigate the truth, through the opposition we received. . . . We meet all kinds

Why England?

In the months and years following the 1898 policy change, many sister missionaries were assigned to labor in England. There are several possible reasons for this: England was ripe for missionary work at the time, particularly from young women native to Utah. For many years, it was the area from which the most converts came—simply put, the field in that country was indeed "white already to harvest" (Doctrine and Covenants 4:4). But it was also ideal because American missionaries serving there required no special language training, and it was an excellent place for Saints with ancestors from England—like many of those early missionaries—to gather genealogical records (Kunz, Calvin S., "A History of Female Missionary Activity in The Church of Jesus Christ of Latter-day Saints, 1830–1898," (master's thesis, Brigham Young University, 1976), 39–40; http://scholarsarchive.byu.edu/cgi/viewcontent.cgi?article=5857&context=etd). Anti-Mormon literature that painted Mormon women as downtrodden slaves was also rampant in England at the time, and real young women from Utah were the most effective speakers against those claims.

---

153 Ibid., 124–25.

of answers, but each day's round finds sunshine and shower, and without one we might not appreciate the other. . . . The Lord is abundantly blessing us in our labors, and although we do not always have clear sailing . . . yet we rejoice in the work."[154]

Like the young sister missionaries of today, Inez Knight was called to the work in large part because of the success of female missionaries who came before her. The prospect of standing on the shoulders of such effective missionaries as Elizabeth McCune and Louisa Barnes Pratt, compounded with the stress of talking about the gospel with hostile strangers, made Inez fearful and anxious at times. But with faith in the Lord, belief in herself, and a great deal of courage, she served an honorable, successful mission. As she demonstrated, each sister missionary has a rich heritage and every reason to be confident as she faces the future with faith.

154 Allen, Inez Knight, "A letter from London," *The Young Woman's Journal*, Vol. 10, No. 4, April 1899, 185.

EPILOGUE
What They Began

Inez Knight and Jennie Brimhall changed the face of Mormon missionary work forever. Thanks in large part to the bright and intelligent women who served as missionaries in the nineteenth century, missionary service became an option for a growing number of single young Mormon women at the turn of the twentieth century. These women then paved the way for many more young women to join the ranks of God's missionary army in the years to come.

For a while, the full implications of the 1898 policy were unclear. Would these lady missionaries be mostly married women, or would single sisters be more practical? How long would they serve? What responsibilities would they have? How might mission presidents use them in missionary work?

In time, the answers became clear. Fewer married women were called to serve alongside their husbands as the years passed. Blanche Woodruff Daynes was serving a mission in England with her husband in June 1900 when she wrote about the struggles of serving as both a missionary and a mother of young children. She wrote: "The other day I made an attempt at tracting; took Donald in his cart, and visited fourteen houses. This was as much as I could do in one day. I am not sure that I did any good, but still I gave a few souls a chance to know a little something of our Gospel. I haven't been out since, and don't know when I shall go again, but it is my intention to do some tracting this summer, if I can with baby."[155]

Although Blanche was willing, the responsibilities of motherhood and the busyness of life as a homemaker in 1900—when basic tasks like washing clothes and cooking were laborious and time-consuming—divided her attention and diminished her effectiveness. Other young mothers suffered the death of children, sometimes due to foreign diseases, while serving missions. These difficulties became apparent to Church leaders and helped lead to the decrease in married sister missionaries. From 1904 to 1908, about 40 percent of female missionaries were married; from 1909 to 1914, fewer than 30 percent were married.[156]

As the number of married women serving as missionaries decreased, the number of single sister missionaries increased rapidly. In 1900, seventeen female missionaries were set apart, making up 2 percent of the total missionary force. By 1910, sisters made up 5 percent of the force. The number of sisters increased steadily over the next decade, partially due to changing demographics in Utah that increased the number of single women and heightened the median age of marriage. In 1918, while many men were fighting in World War I, women made up 38 percent of the missionary force, a percentage not exceeded again until World War II. In 1945, women made up over half of the total missionary force. The percentage of female missionaries dropped after World War II ended, but the total number of female missionaries held steady or increased in subsequent years.[157]

---

155 Blanche W. Daynes, "Our Girls," *The Young Woman's Journal*, Vol. 11, No. 6, June 1900, 279.

156 See Missionary Registers, Books C and D, Church Archives. Quoted in McBride, Matthew, "Do You Believe in Lady Missionaries?" June 5, 2014; http://www.juvenileinstructor.org/do-you-believe-lady-missionaries/; accessed March 4, 2015.

157 See Payne, Tally S., "'Our Wise and Prudent Women'": Twentieth-Century Trends in Female Missionary Service," in *New Scholarship on Latter-day Saint Women in the Twentieth Century* (2005), 127.

An increased number of women in the mission field led to a dramatic cultural change in the Church that received mixed reviews. In 1915, a leader in the Eastern States Mission wrote: "The idea of having lady missionaries is new in this mission, but is no longer an experiment. The faithful labors of these sisters have gone far in making the mission what it is today. Neither their devotion can be questioned, nor their industry criticized. Their services have been of great value in tracting, in which capacity they are generally well received. Great credit is due them for the number of cottage meetings they have been able to arrange for and hold, and they have held some very successful street meetings."[158]

Later that year, a persuasive article defending the role of women in the mission field was published in the *Improvement Era* under the title "Do You Believe in Lady Missionaries?" In it, the author acknowledged a disparity of views among the Latter-day Saints: "Do you believe in lady missionaries? Quite a division of opinion prevails among the people on this question. . . . Why is this the case? Do you believe in sending out young women to labor in the mission field? Or should mission work be done solely by the Priesthood?"[159]

The female missionaries' success spoke for itself, and President James A. McRae, of the Colorado Mission in 1904, wrote, "I consider women missionaries a valuable aid in the work of spreading truth. They seem to get access to homes that cannot be opened by the Elders. They seem to change many of the prevailing opinions regarding the [treatment] of women in Utah. They answer the question that is often asked of us, 'What do the women of Utah say about the system of religion, and are they as contented as you say they are?'"[160]

---

158 "Messages from the Missions," *Improvement Era*, Vol. 18, No. 5, March 1915, 457.

159 "Do You Believe in Lady Missionaries?," *Improvement Era*, Vol. 17, No. 1, November 1915, 144.

160 McMurrin, Joseph W., "Lady Missionaries," *Young Woman's Journal*, December 1904, 540.

Thousands more women served throughout the twentieth century. In 1901, the *Woman's Exponent* wrote, "President Lyman, late of the European Mission, has in all soberness declared 'that the lady missionary is no longer an experiment, but an unqualified success.' In the early dawn of the twentieth century this fact has been demonstrated to the world. What will the future unfold? Will her career end here? Nay! Broad avenues, today unexplored will be open for her earnest efforts to teach the principles of purity and truth."[161]

This prediction has proven true, especially since President Thomas S. Monson's historic 2012 announcement. This change of policy instigated a second wave of female missionaries that flooded the mission field in the wake created by a century's worth of successful sisters.

As the lessons of the past and the hope of the future combine, missionaries' testimonies of Christ are magnified more than at any time in the history of the Church or, indeed, the world. Thanks in part to a vibrant missionary force made up of both men and women, the gospel of Jesus Christ will, as Joseph Smith said, "Go forth boldly, nobly, and independent, till it has penetrated every continent, visited every clime, swept every country, and sounded in every ear, till the purposes of God shall be accomplished, and the Great Jehovah shall say the work is done."[162]

---

161 Alder, Lydia D. "Thoughts on Missionary Work," *Woman's Exponent*, Vol. 30, No. 3 August 1, 1901, 22.

162 *Teachings of Presidents of the Church: Joseph Smith* (2011), 135–47.

ABOUT THE AUTHOR

Breanna Bennett Olaveson is a writer, a reporter, a researcher, and a lover of all good stories. Few things bring her more joy than telling another person's story authentically, positively, and accurately, and when she learned about the first sister missionaries in the Church, she knew she'd hit a storytelling gold mine. Her favorite people to read and write about are those who have remarkable stories no one has heard but that everyone should hear—people like the women in "Sweet Is the Work." She lives in Utah with her husband and three children.